The Trivial Life

The Trivial Life

ESCAPING THE DEFAULT MODE OF THE HUMAN HEART

Jason S. Lancaster

Shepherd Press
Wapwallopen, Pennsylvania

The Trivial Life: Escaping the Default Mode of the Human Heart

© 2020 Jason S. Lancaster

ISBN:
Print: 978-1-63342-195-0
epub: 978-1-63342-196-7
Kindle: 978-1-63342-197-4

Shepherd Press
P.O. Box 24
Wapwallopen, PA 18660

www.shepherdpress.com
http://thetriviallife.com

Typography by **documen**

—— ACKNOWLEDGMENTS ——

To my brothers and sisters from Providence Church,
Evanston Bible Fellowship, and Village Bible
Church, where we joyfully spur one another on
to live the Weighty Life.

To Fran Taylor, for her outstanding editing skills,
clever insights, and wise suggestions.

To Trudi Sowers, for her diligent reading
and keen eye for perfection.

To Shepherd Press for giving me the opportunity
to write on matters of the heart.

To my wife and kids, who encourage me
to live for the glory of God.

APPRECIATIONS

We all want our lives to count for something bigger than us. Jason Lancaster has provided an important guide pointing us to that end! *The Trivial Life* is a delightful, soul-stirring read that helps followers of Jesus expose and trade our often-trivial ambitions in exchange for something far more significant—the weighty life. Jason's transparent, humorous, and personal stories, coupled with thoughtful biblical reflections, are valuable for all Christians who want to impact the community and world around them.

Eric Rivera Lead Pastor, The Brook, Chicago

"Your perspective determines your priorities—and your priorities determine your practices" —*Anonymous*. I heard this quote and then thought maybe it's more like "Your priorities determine your perspective—and your perspective determines your practices." It's like, "But seek first the kingdom of God and his righteousness, and all these things will be added to you." This sounds like the "weighty norms" Jason Lancaster writes about in his book *The Trivial Life: Escaping the Default Mode of the Human Heart*. Lancaster has given us a gift of biblical clarity. He not only shows us the city on the hill but gives us clear directions on how to get there. Biblical; practical; life-giving; and hopeful. Now that is a book I want to read—and I have—in Lancaster's *The Trivial Life*.

Rodney L. Cooper Ph.D. Kenneth and Jean Hansen Professor of Discipleship and Leadership, Gordon Conwell Theological Seminary

In a handful of decades, most all of us will have reached our life's end, or will soon. The great question is how we'll live between this day and that. Will we look back on a string of self-absorbed days that yielded little of lasting value? Or—despite our fears and frailties—will we have given ourselves to things of lasting value? Jason Lancaster helps us to see and to feel what we really want. Best of all, he reminds us of the eternal weight of each of our day's small choices to love God and neighbor.

Jedd Medefind President, Christian Alliance for Orphans

The Trivial Life puts words to paper of what it really feels like to be a Christian but still wrestle with the flesh. Jason Lancaster dives into what it takes to live and breathe a life of weight (not to be confused with heavy) and truth. With grace and boldness, these words will urge you on in your faith.

Chelsea Kay Hurst Author of *Your Own Beautiful* and *Above All Else: 60 Devotions for Young Women*

You want to live for something more than the trivial life? Then you'll need to look toward home. Jason Lancaster has been looking toward home for thirty years, and we can all learn a lot from his example. But this book has only one Hero, and it's not Jason. I'm thankful for how he makes much of Jesus in this challenging and compelling book.

Collin Hansen Editorial Director for The Gospel Coalition and author of *Blind Spots: Becoming a Courageous, Compassionate, and Commissioned Church*

Run, don't walk, to get *The Trivial Life* by Dr. Jason Lancaster. Life is too short to spend it on the mundane. Jason calls us to step up our game. You will find real help in this book.

Brian Bird Writer-Executive Producer—When Calls the Heart

Jason Lancaster reminds us in his book, *The Trivial Life*, that "unless intentional action is taken you are always going to lean in the direction of pursuing that which is trivial." Making conscious decisions about how we will spend the time and energy of our lives will cause us to invest in others in productive ways. This book will help you determine priorities for your life. I highly recommend it to you.

Mike Huckabee Former Governor of Arkansas

CONTENTS

Bowling is trivial

Not for professionals or for a recreational activity
among friends and family . . .

Play on!

But it crosses the line when the everyday man or
woman becomes captivated and consumed with
bowling.

Imagine spending hours online and in the
store researching the perfect ball with just the
right weight, color, feel, and even fit for your
personality.

There's the alien ball, the spider ball, the
warrior ball, and the rhino ball in all shades
imaginable, including neon and multi-colored. But
one ball is not enough, as you need at least five
to ten balls to match the oil consistency of each
unique lane. After receiving the immaculate ball,
you must get it drilled for the ideal placement of
the three holes based upon your grip, the center
of gravity of the ball, and your unique roll. Don't
mess this up or you will destroy your game.

The clothing is just as important for a strategic advantage and to make a fashion statement. The pants have to stretch and flex while giving off the groovy cool look of hipness. You are always on your phone looking for the newest designs of shirts and hoping to win a few online auctions for the vintage styles. And shoes, they are the key to take that victory! You can easily spend hundreds to find the shoes that slide just right with the interchangeable sole to match your stride. Take all the gear and shove it in a high dollar roller bag, then you are almost good to go.

One last crucial piece you have to acquire is an awesome coach to up your game. After years of trial and error working through a few, you think you have finally landed on the perfect coach. Now you are set for tournaments, meet ups, and multiple leagues that take you away from your work, family, and friends. Your phone alerts are set to update you on the score's professionals roll and what's happening in the world of bowling. Your mind is consumed with bowling, your screen saver is bowling, your ring tone is pins crashing, your conversations are all about bowling; and when you go to bed and wake up, you are enraptured with bowling.

THIS IS PSYCHO BOWLING. Surely this person has gone a little crazy and fails to see the consequences of his obsession. Not only is he neglecting work and relationships but he's failing to engage other important aspects of life. He is wasting his life on that which is meaningless and pointless. No one wants to imitate this person because he's living the epitome of the trivial life to the exclusion of weightier things.

The trivial life of the extreme bowler stands in stark contrast to a time when I had a "bowling ball" in my lap—it was actually someone's head. Once I took a quick trip to Haiti to visit a husband-and-wife team who lead an orphanage called HIS Home for Children. Hal is the executive director overseeing the business aspects of the orphanage along with its thirty-five staff members. His wife, Chris, is the caregiver. Her medical skills, combined with her social work and mothering background, make her the ideal nurturer. They don't commute but actually live at the orphanage. It's their home, and they treat the kids as their own. Even after long days of tending to the needs of the children, they have been known to wake up at night to dispense medicine or switch out an IV of a sick child. It's a lot to keep up with 120 kids!

During my short stay, I went with Chris to help her give haircuts to children with special needs. My job was to hold the kids in my lap as she cut their hair down to the scalp. It was the hydrocephalic kids that were the hardest to handle. Chris told me to be careful because their heads were as heavy as bowling balls. She wasn't joking. These little ones had huge heads that literally felt like a bowling ball in my lap. The condition, sometimes referred to as "water on the brain," causes massive swelling of the head. The necks of these children are in extreme pain because their heads sometimes weigh about four times that of their bodies. But they still needed haircuts, so, with much love and compassion, Chris patiently shaved their heads.

I had not been in Haiti long and had just met Hal and Chris, but I was absolutely sure that the work they were doing was not trivial. In fact, their endeavors were not only important but crucial for the children to survive and thrive.

My two examples cross the spectrum of extremes: the trivial pursuit of the psycho bowler with his bowling balls and the non-trivial pursuits of Hal and Chris with the bowling-ball heads of children. If I pinned you down and asked where you land on the spectrum of trivial matters, would you fall closer . . . to bowling, or to bowling-ball heads? Most can see the nobility of caring for those suffering; you long to move in the direction of pursuing those things in life with greater meaning and purpose. But if you did an honest assessment of what you do with your time, thoughts, and actions, you might be closer to the bowler than you would like to admit.

A helpful assessment comes in your responses to a set of extremes. Evaluate the following list and consider where you would land on the spectrum between that which is trivial and that which is important. No one is as good as he wants to be or as bad as he can be, but all fall somewhere on the spectrum. Where do your responses fall between that which is trivial and that which is meaningful?

TRIVIAL	MEANINGFUL
Bowling	Bowling-ball heads
Self-Centered Withdrawal	Engaging Relationships
Materialism	Generosity
Gossip	Encouragement
Fantasy	Reality
Slacking at work	Diligence at work
Addicted to Technology	Utilizing Technology
Sports Obsessed	Sports in Perspective
Pornography	Sexual Purity
Crushing Power	Servant Leadership
Discontent	Content
Lazy	Helpful
Frenzied Grind	Peaceful Pace

Once again, this is a spectrum. You may utilize technology for good things, but too many times your phone may consume every spare minute of your life. In addition, you may physically be present, caring for all your family responsibilities, while your mind fantasizes about a new spouse and a new life. And curling up with a good book or watching TV can easily turn into hours of avoiding certain relationships and commitments.

Now, if you did an honest assessment of what you do with your time, thoughts, and actions, would you be closer to the bowler than you would like to admit?

Why does your life (and mine) often trend toward that which is trivial? *Because the default mode of the human heart is bent toward triviality.* Unless intentional action is taken, you are always going to lean in the direction of pursuing that which is trivial. Just as your computer settings will operate under their default mode unless directed by you to do otherwise, so will your life. It's not hard to pursue triviality because you have naturally done it your whole life.

But what if there were some kind of work-around, intentional reset or deliberate action on your part to move away from triviality, to a life of meaning and purpose? What if you could push back against the default mode of the human heart so that you could live a life pursuing that which is significant and important? Here's the good news: You are not destined to live a life of futility but a life of consequence as you engage the critical aspects of life on a day-to-day basis.

The premise behind escaping the trivial life is that God is not a trivial God, nor did He create humans for a life of triviality. Though we have all gone in search of our own ways down the road of rebellious triviality, God has intervened through the person of Jesus Christ. Through His life, death, and resurrection, Jesus delivers those through faith who have been held captive to sinful triviality their whole lives. Jesus did not come to give you tips and tricks for meaningful living, but to overhaul and restructure your life from the inside out. The results are a God-consumed life that starts to form and grow as you become more and more like Jesus Christ who perfectly embodied the God-consumed life. Not only was He the perfect God-man but His one aim was to glorify God the Father in all that He did. Now, through faith in Jesus, you can live a God-consumed life in all that you do to the glory of the Father.

The opposite of the trivial life is what I want to call the *weighty life*. Don't think in terms of physical weight but along the lines of things that are so important and valuable in life that they carry much "weight." In the Bible, the concept of God's glory is sometimes referred to in terms of weightiness. The term *glory* or *Kabod* in the Hebrew literally means "heavy" or "weighty." When God is considered in all of His character and attributes, it could be called His glory. You could say that God in His fullness is "heavy" or "weighty"; His magnitude and worth far outweigh all else.

As you move away from the Trivial Life to the Weighty Life, you will live in such a way that brings attention to the value and worth of God. Psalm 86:9 says,

> *All the nations you have made shall come*
> *and worship before you, O Lord,*
> *and shall **glorify** your name*

(Emphasis above is mine.) Honor and praise come to God from people who acknowledge Him in all of His glory and weightiness. Psalm 22:23 calls,

> *You who fear the Lord, praise him!*
> *All you offspring of Jacob, glorify him,*
> *and stand in awe of him, all you offspring of Israel!*

God is distinct from His people, and they are to praise and ascribe glory and weight to Him alone. The weighty life showcases God in all of His perfections and glory.

A New Testament expression of the weighty life comes from 1 Corinthians 10:31: "So, whether you eat or drink, or whatever you do, do all to the glory of God." This verse is more than a nice slogan, bumper sticker or refrigerator magnet. The weighty life will be God-consumed and seek to honor God and bring Him glory in all aspects of life. Colossians 3:17 comes into play as well: "And whatever you do, in word or deed, do everything in the name of the Lord Jesus, giving thanks to God the Father through Him." The weighty life is God-focused and Jesus-centered in word, thought and deed.

The aim of the Christian life is to be transformed by grace so that you move further and further away from the trivial life into a full expression of the weighty life. If you find yourself closer to the trivial life of the bowler than the weighty life of Hal and Chris, you don't have to be discouraged. Perhaps all you need is the slightest push to start moving in the direction of living a life filled with meaning and purpose. Think of a parent helping a little child release her first bowling ball down the lane. The ball moves so slowly but eventually it gets there. And sometimes it's a strike. May your heavenly Father use the following pages to gently move you in the direction of the weighty life so that you will not only find meaning and purpose but ultimately bring Him glory.

CHAPTER
1

Heart

At one time, my phone was set to receive text alerts from two different entities. The first one is a travel guru who can sniff out and spot a travel deal better than anyone else. When he finds one, he sends out an alert to all his subscribers to jump on the deal ASAP. His texts can include round-trip airfare from Los Angeles to New York for $80, hotel specials for free nights in some of the most luxurious places in the world, offers for cheap cruises, or vacation packages around the world to exotic locations of adventure. These alerts hit my phone about twice a week. I was eager to see what he would come up with next—maybe an exciting deal I could jump on for an adventure.

My phone was also set to receive alerts and texts from an organization looking for temporary homes for children while their parents were in a hard season of life. It's not adoption or foster care but a temporary solution of a safe place for children as their parents make it through difficulties. I would get a text looking for a home for a nine-year-old girl for a week as her dad undergoes surgery. The placement may be for two kids for a couple of weeks as their parents find temporary housing and get off the streets. These alerts would hit my phone about once or twice a week reaching out for help during a difficult season.

These weekly texts seem to offer two different opportunities. Let's say I came to you for advice to see which one I should accept. I have two weeks free in my schedule, and the family is in a good, normal rhythm with the kids doing all right and marriage going pretty well.

The travel deal is a two week stay in Cancun, Mexico, at an all-inclusive five-star resort with airfare, tips, and transfers included for two people at $1,000. It's not a time-share scheme but a straight-up deal and about a third of the price of what it would normally cost. The other "deal" is to watch seven-year-old twins for a couple of weeks while their mom interviews for jobs and finds permanent housing so they won't have to keep living in a shelter. What should I do? You spell it out for me. I can relax in the sun, snorkel, eat lots of good food, and enjoy my life. Or, I can choose to add stress, care for others, and disrupt my family for two weeks.

There are times for vacation and fun. And there are times for stepping up and intervening in a crisis. But, more often than not, if we are honest, most of our time is spent in the direction of self rather than the direction of others. And, if we are really honest, most of our days are spent pampering ourselves rather than serving others. Something is seriously out of whack.

THE HEART IS THE PROBLEM

The heart is mentioned over 900 times in the Bible and 77 times alone in the book of Proverbs. Often when the Bible talks about your heart, it refers to the core of who you are. It's your thoughts, motives, emotions, personality, and the spiritual part of your makeup. Your heart is basically who you are. Proverbs 27:19 puts it like this,

> *As in water face reflects face,*
> *so the heart of man reflects the man.*

When we talk about getting to know someone better, we mean that we are getting to know their heart and who they really are at the core.

One of the more well-known verses on the heart is Proverbs 4:23, "Above all else, guard your heart, for it is the wellspring of life." It's as if all of your life is bursting forth from your heart. If one were to explain what you do, it would all come back to the heart. It's in the heart where you can see your bent toward triviality.

Why are you lacking contentment when you have so much? The heart. Why do you meditate or fantasize about winning the lottery? The heart. Why do you secretly hope that others crash and burn just a bit? The heart. Why do you fear others and their opinions of you? The heart. Why do you just want to be left alone to live life on your own terms?

The heart. Why do you do what you do? The heart. Your life is springing forth from your heart because your heart is the core of who you are.

I don't particularly like this reality as I often think that factors outside of me cause me to act in trivial and foolish ways. When I was a young child, I stole a piece of candy from the local Tom Thumb grocery store. Why would I do that? Because the candy was there in plain sight. If they didn't want me to take it, then they should lock it up. It's not my fault.

Through elementary school I would hit my brother, kick a classmate, and even slap the dog. Why would I do such things? Because they were being irritating. It wasn't my fault! If they weren't so annoying, then they would not be hit, kicked or slapped. It was clearly their problem.

As a teenager my greed grew, rage replaced anger, and sexual immorality was the new kid on the block. Lust was out of control, but it wasn't my fault. If girls did not want me to look at them in that way, then they should dress appropriately at school, and grown women should not undress in all those magazines I looked at. The problem was always outside of me and never inside my heart.

Contrary to my belief, the Bible is pretty clear that the problem is inside rather than outside. The heart is messed up, even twisted and sick.

> *The heart is deceitful above all things,*
> *and desperately sick;*
> *who can understand it?*

> (Jeremiah 17:9)

Many commencement speakers encourage graduates to "follow their hearts." Not always the best idea. When a Disney movie tells you to trust your heart, just yell out right there in the theater, "Don't do it!" The heart naturally defaults toward triviality, leading to a variety of unwise decisions and missed opportunities.

A New Heart

In order to escape the trivial life, the "desperately sick" heart that we are all born with must be removed and replaced with a brand-new heart. When we confess our own sin and repent of our own wrongdoing and put our faith in Jesus, we are changed and given a new heart and a new Spirit. Ezekiel puts it in these amazing words:

> *And I will give you a new heart, and a new spirit I will put within you. And I will remove the heart of stone from your flesh and give you a heart of flesh. And I will put my Spirit within you, and cause you to walk in my statutes and be careful to obey my rules.*
> (Ezekiel 36:26–27)

Before conversion, believers had hard hearts against God, but now they are new, soft, and malleable. The new heart, filled with the Holy Spirit, wants to obey and worship Jesus.

My supernatural heart transplant was performed on me when I was at the height of triviality and sin. After finishing my freshman year in college, I needed to make some money over the summer. A camp in Missouri called Kanakuk was a Christian sports camp and they toured college campuses interviewing potential counselors. Since I played collegiate tennis and was a cultural Christian, I thought it sounded all right. One of the questions the interviewer asked was whether or not I had pre-marital sex. I lied and said "No." Then he asked me what book of the Bible I had been studying. Since I did not know the Bible at all I said, "Paul." (FYI: Paul is not a book in the Bible.) He followed up by asking me what part of Paul, and I said, "All of Paul." A few weeks later, to my surprise, I got hired.

Summer arrives, and I show up to do my counseling duties. All the other counselors are speaking about Jesus, leading kids to Christ, and discipling them to be world changers. Okay, whatever, I'm here to get paid and meet girls. To my shame, I did just that. Here I was fully immersed in my trivial life of deception, immorality, and greed; then, one night, I had open-heart surgery while I was fully awake. A leader was presenting the gospel and I was literally cut to the heart and became undone. Conviction exploded within me, I ran outside, and I broke down with heavy sobs. I repented of my sins and put my faith in the Lord Jesus Christ to cleanse me and make me new.

NEW HEART, OLD STRUGGLES

For the past twenty plus years I have been a pastor. For the past twenty plus years I have been in and out of counseling. Counselors love me because I'm the classic blame shifter who is easy to spot. "What brings you in today?" My wife has issues. "Why do you think you struggle with anxiety?" Because my seven kids are driving me crazy. "Why are you so filled with fear and anger?" Because my congregation keeps picking on me. It's like I'm still a child in a grown man's body. The problem is still out there and not inside of me. When will I learn?

Deep inside my regenerated heart, something is still off. Conversion doesn't eliminate the battle and struggle with sin. The Bible uses terms such as "the flesh" (Galatians 5:13) or "indwelling sin" (Romans 7:17). There is an internal war going on within the believer between "the desires of the flesh" and "the desires of the Spirit" (Galatians 5:16–17). The "flesh" is the old "me-centered" sinful way of doing life. The "Spirit" is the new Christ-centered way of doing life. The war is real, and you can feel it on a daily basis: nagging fears, unhindered anger, unchecked desires, and ongoing relational turmoil. Even though your heart is no longer enslaved to sin, it still has a propensity to dabble in your old patterns of life. And if you fail to engage in the war, then your heart will keep defaulting toward triviality.

Let me express the battle in a non-traditional way. There was once a book and a movie called *World War Z*. The *Z* stands for zombies, which are the living dead walking around. The plot has a lot to do with a war between the living and the living-dead zombies, hence, *World War Z*. In a sense, every Christian has a "world war Z" going on within.

Here's some zombie theology. Your old self along with its passions and desires has been killed (Galatians 5:24). This means that your old sinful way of living the trivial life no longer has to dominate you because your old self has been killed at the cross. Romans 6:6, ". . . knowing this, that our old self was crucified with Him, in order that our body of sin might be done away with, so that we would no longer be slaves to sin" (NASB). Yet, your old self acts like a zombie. It's dead, yet it tries to live on and rule your life again. That is why there is a "world war Z" within.

This internal war is described in James 4:1–2: "What is the source of quarrels and conflicts among you? Is not the source your pleasures that *wage war in your members*? You lust and do not have; so you commit murder. You are envious and cannot obtain; so you fight and quarrel. You do not have because you do not ask" (NASB, italics mine). When we don't get what we want, our flesh tends to strike. It's not what we ultimately want but something warring within as Paul says in Romans 7:22–23: "For I joyfully concur with the law of God in the inner man, but I see a different law in the members of my body, waging war against the law of my mind and making me a prisoner of the law of sin which is in my members" (NASB). As believers, we truly want to live the weighty life, but the flesh is always trying to pull us back into the default mode of triviality. That is why we must diligently fight.

Some Christians act as if there is no struggle or war, as if it's just a matter of positive thinking and claiming the victory. But not me. I feel like I'm in a battle on a daily basis. I once told my congregation that if they knew my twisted temptations, there would be a mob riot to run me out of town. And if we were all aware of their temptations, we would lock some of them up in the prayer room to cast out demons. But there is no need for mob riots or exorcisms as we are simply facing temptations that are common to humanity. The good news is that, in this battle, God always provides a way of escape. This should give us hope to stay in the battle in order to live in His victory.

GUARD YOUR HEART

This brings us back to Proverbs 4:23: "Above all else, guard your heart, for everything you do flows from it." (NIV). To guard and keep your heart means to protect what comes in and goes out. You have to constantly be on guard and keep your heart with all vigilance because it's the command center for all your words, actions, and desires.

John Flavel, an old Puritan pastor, used the example of guarding your heart like a besieged garrison with enemies on the outside and treacherous citizens on the inside. The imagery is dated, but the idea is good, so let me run with it in a modern equivalent.

Before I was a follower of Christ, I had an unguarded and rebellious heart that engaged in all types of trivial activities. My heart was like a frat house that partied hard (no offense to good wholesome fraternities). I had no restraints on the anger and foul language that came out and that I let in. I had no guard on the amounts of sexual immorality that I expressed and invited in. Greed came out of my heart and freely welcomed new greedy ideas. There was freedom for sin to come out of my corrupt heart and to come in to corrupt it even more. The trivial life abounded.

Then Jesus demolished and removed my frat-house heart and gave me a new "White House" heart. The imagery I moved from was an everything-goes frat house to a heavily guarded "White House" (one of the most guarded homes in the country). My heart is now purified and the Holy Spirit lives in me and enables me to guard my heart (house). By God's grace, I am now to be vigilant in guarding what comes in and out of my heart (house). I must not let in sexually immoral images. I must keep out offers of greed and anxiety. They may knock but they aren't getting in.

I must also keep my heart guarded against rebellion within. It's as if I see my heart filled with these rooms of indwelling sin. One room is for anxiety, another for sexual immorality, and another for greed, and on and on. They often want to deceive me and get out and run free. That is why I must be brutal with them and bring the heat of the gospel and put them to death (Romans 8:13). Greed will come out of his room and roam the halls and tell me that guys my age are cashing in and I'm missing out. Then I see an ad for a "Rich Dad, Poor Dad" seminar, which is basically telling me that I'm the lame, poor dad. The combination of the internal and external attacks can cause greed to spill out all over the place. That's why I must guard my heart both internally and externally.

If you are a believer, your heart is now purified and the Holy Spirit lives in you and enables you to guard your house (heart). By God's grace, you can now be vigilant in guarding what comes in and out of your heart in your words, actions, and desires.

—Words

Proverbs 15:28: "The heart of the righteous ponders how to answer, but the mouth of the wicked pours out evil things."

The heart of a wise person speaks with timely, appropriate, and wise words. But the opposite is seen in the fool who gushes out junk and triviality. Your words reveal your heart condition. If your words are foolish and hurt others, you don't have a word problem—you have a heart problem. Jesus said in Luke 6:45, "The good person out of the good treasure of his heart produces good, and the evil person out of his evil treasure produces evil, for out of the abundance of the heart his mouth speaks." If you tend to be cutting and sarcastic toward others, it might be helpful to explore what is lurking inside your heart that causes you to go off.

—Actions

Your actions are derived from your heart. Following a discussion with the Pharisees, Jesus put it like this in Mark 7:20–23, in the context of what defiles a person, not clean or unclean foods but the heart:

And he said, "What comes out of a person is what defiles him. For from within, out of the heart of man, come evil thoughts, sexual immorality, theft, murder, adultery, coveting, wickedness, deceit, sensuality, envy, slander, pride, foolishness. All these evil things come from within, and they defile a person."

The heart is the root issue of all these evil and trivial behaviors. Again, what is going on inside your heart that causes you to act in ways you later regret?

—Desires

Proverbs 6:25: "Do not desire her beauty in your heart, and do not let her capture you with her eyelashes." This is a father instructing his son how to avoid adultery. He warns against letting the imagination go wild in his heart. The words of Jesus in Matthew 5:28 concur: "But I say to you that everyone who looks at a woman with lustful intent has already committed adultery with her in his heart." It's much easier to let the mind and imagination go wild than to guard against the temptations that happen in the heart. An unguarded heart will always go back to its trivial default mode unless guarded on a daily basis.

EXPLORATION OF THE HEART

One aspect of guarding your heart is having an awareness of what's going on inside. Often, we can see what's coming at us, but we fail to see how we are processing life internally and dishing it back out. Self-awareness in our culture is called emotional intelligence or EQ. It's the ability to know yourself and how you relate to others. It's an awareness of how you come across. Do you realize how you come across? Ask someone close to you, "How do others view me?" (Husbands, I dare you to ask your wife.) Some people are said to have low EQ, like the father who criticizes his kids for being on electronics way too much while he can't even go to the bathroom without his phone. Or, it's the nitpicky and gossipy coworker who fails to see his own incompetence and laziness. You and I both have certain blind spots that we are unaware of or that we simply ignore. It's this lack of self-awareness that will hinder you from escaping the trivial life and moving toward the weighty life

My hope and prayer is that the following chapters will give you some insight into your ongoing heart struggles so that you will see a way of escape. Going forward, we will explore the *visioneering* process of the heart that leads to the trivial life rooted in false worship and is often creatively absurd. For good measure, we will look at someone who went all in with the trivial life and had the skill, money, and power to pull it off—but found it wanting. Then we will turn our attention to liberation from the trivial life here on this earth while we wait to be with Jesus forever in the eternal weighty life. Escaping provides a fresh start to establish a new way of living based upon the elements and virtues of the weighty life. Finally, we will take a look at real life and specific weighty norms that characterize followers of Jesus.

THE TENDER AND SKILLED HEART SURGEON

One summer, my wife and I watched a TV documentary called *NY Med*. It was a reality show that revealed the emotions and the grind inside a variety of New York hospitals. Often the storyline surrounded some type of heart surgery. The surgeon would meet with the patient and tell him all the problems with his heart: clots, disease, failing, etc. What the surgeon would often say was, "It looks bad, but I am not going to know how bad until I open you up." This was always a setup because, sure enough, in the next scene when the patient was opened up, it was worse than expected. Sometimes the heart had additional problems; other times blood started to hemorrhage out, and sometimes the patient's heart even stopped beating for a while. Eventually, the surgeon came through, the patient lived, and everyone praised and hugged the surgeon.

Though you have a brand-new heart when you trust Jesus as your Savior, there are still ongoing complications that need to be dealt with. Invite the Great Physician to open you up. Your issues and junk will likely gush out, and it might be worse than you thought. But don't be discouraged! I know the feeling. In some of my lower pastoral moments, I become cynical and feel as if most people don't really change. And in my darkest personal moments, I wonder if *I* even change. But I don't want to stay there because the tender and skilled Physician can deal with whatever comes out of our hearts and He is ready to heal. I'm going to go as far as to say, "Expect to change." Expect a big God to change you. He loves you and is ready to pour out His grace and mercy so that you can escape the trivial life and live in the freedom of the weighty life.

CHAPTER
2

— Visioneering —

I like the made-up word *visioneering*. It's a combination of vision and engineering. It captures the concept of having a vision and a plan to pull it off. You are probably a visioneering person. You have a vision you want to accomplish, and a plan to make it reality. Usually, visioneering is used in positive ways as if the dream you have for your life is good and, all you need is the right blueprint to make it happen. But motives are tricky, and, if you were honest, you might see that some of your visioneering is quite trivial.

Here is a common visioneering scenario. Most married people eventually want to buy a house. It may be cool to live in the cramped urban core of the city, but, as the family expands, most want to land in a house. It's such an exciting visioneering process made of dreams for the perfect house and the details to acquire it. Even Christians have these visioneering scenarios but with a "kingdom" mindset. A couple will want to buy a home and even a BIG home because they want to be more hospitable, host a small group, and accommodate church events. In fact, they would even like to have a spare room for missionaries who come to town. And who knows, they may even fill the many rooms up one day with adopted children.

These are good visioneering scenarios. But it makes me wonder, are people just saying these things to justify a large house? Once the dream home comes to fruition, is it really used in a way that matches the original kingdom intent? Maybe, maybe not.

MOTIVES ARE TRICKY

I spent more than twenty years with college students helping them visioneer their lives. The question they usually ask is, "What is God's will for my life?" They are looking for specific answers on majors, careers, and mates to match their gifting, calling, and preferences. They are begging God for a vision. But like the rest of us, their reception of God's will is often reinterpreted in terms that best suit the desired outcomes of comfort and ease. It's as if God says one thing in His Word, but by the time it filters through the heart, it's far from the original intent. Something seems to be lost in translation.

Here are a couple of verses, among many, that should be thrown into the visioneering mix but are often hanging out on the spiritual sidelines. Jesus said to His followers, "If anyone would come after me, let him deny himself and take up his cross and follow me" (Matthew 16:24). This seems to indicate that the path of following Jesus will be filled with difficulties and perhaps even death. The apostle Paul pushes as well, writing, "Let each of you look not only to his own interests, but also to the interests of others" (Philippians 2:4). The intent of the passage is for you to serve others along the same lines that Christ has served you. Put the two passages together and it's clear that, no matter the minutiae of the visioneering process, at the very least it should include some form of sacrificial allegiance to Christ and servant orientation to others. These are just two basic verses; God's Word has a lot more to throw in the visioneering mix.

Most of us know verses like these but we are also pretty good at tricking ourselves. It's like the recent college grad who told me that he wanted to make so much money—millions—that he could support missionaries. Perhaps he is visioneering the weighty life, but maybe it's just the trivial life couched in spiritual language. Let's wait and see how it turns out.

And that's just it; we can't see the way things will turn out. Maybe this recent grad will hit his stride and cash in for the Lord in sacrificial ways that serve others. Or, maybe he will hit midlife still investing in one scheme after another, hoping to finally hit it big and change the world. Who am I to question motives, but it seems to be wise to at least ask the question. What exactly are you trying to build? Spell it out. Go into detail. Lay out the plan.

WHAT EXACTLY ARE YOU TRYING TO BUILD?

One of the most trivial images I have ever read in the Bible is about craftsmen building idols (Isaiah 44). It's as if the

Lord mocks the visioneering process. It's quite humorous while also extremely convicting.

> *The ironsmith takes a cutting tool and works it over*
> *the coals. He fashions it with hammers and works*
> *it with his strong arm. He becomes hungry, and his*
> *strength fails; he drinks no water and is faint.*
>
> (Isaiah 44:12)

The Bible speaks of God creating and forming humans; He fashions them (Isaiah 43:1). Not to be outdone, this idol maker assumes a godlike role as he "fashions" an idol, but the poor guy is getting hungry, tired, and losing his mojo.

> *The carpenter stretches a line; he marks it out with a*
> *pencil. He shapes it with planes and marks it with a*
> *compass. He shapes it into the figure of a man, with*
> *the beauty of a man, to dwell in a house.*
>
> (Isaiah 44:13)

The idol maker is a skilled carpenter who carves out a little dude from the wood and sticks him in a temple.

The absurdity of idol making now takes center stage as the carpenter uses the leftover wood to warm himself and heat up his dinner.

> *Then it becomes fuel for a man. He takes a part of*
> *it and warms himself; he kindles a fire and bakes*
> *bread. Also he makes a god and worships it; he*

*makes it an idol and falls down before it. Half of
it he burns in the fire. Over the half he eats meat;
he roasts it and is satisfied. Also he warms himself
and says, "Aha, I am warm, I have seen the fire!"
And the rest of it he makes into a god, his idol, and
falls down to it and worships it. He prays to it and
says, "Deliver me, for you are my god!"*

(Isaiah 44:15–17)

Wood from the same tree is used for heat, food and worship. Absurd!

Who would ever do something that stupid? That's exactly what Israel was supposed to think of the futility of idol worship, but they had a history of worshipping false gods and idols. Even after God delivered them out of Egypt, they were bowing down to a golden calf (Exodus 32). During the cycles of the Judges they would be delivered by God from their enemies but then go right back to worshipping the idols of their enemies. The idolatry continued on and on until God finally kicked them out of the promised land. Enough is enough.

You and I have a history as well. We may not be building a little statue to worship, but the carving of our idols can be just as real. It's like we are little gods visioneering what we are going to build on our terms. I determine and create what I need for my life. I determine and create what I desire. I determine and create what will make me happy. I determine and create what will make me secure. I determine and create what will give me comfort. I determine and create what will give me control. Modern idol makers are just as trivial as ancient idol makers. And lest you think this language is too strong for New Testament believers, consider the ending of 1 John 5:21: "Little children, keep yourselves from idols."

ENDLESS UPGRADES

When I was a teenager, I worked my first job at an Arby's restaurant. One year I agreed to work during the Christmas break. My motivation for working during the Christmas break was so that I could buy a brand new twelve-inch Cerwin Vega woofer to put in my 1982 Oldsmobile and pump the music. I wanted the whole block to not only hear me coming but feel me coming. But it wasn't loud enough. I soon wanted two fifteen-inch woofers, so I discarded my hard-earned twelve-inch woofer to the junk pile. This began the process of upgrading my stereo system and speakers for the next few years. I would get pumped with the new acquisitions, but it was soon insufficient and left me wanting more. Each purchase provided that short-term high, but it quickly fizzled out until the next upgrade.

This upgrade mentality still plays out with our phones, careers, cars, spouses, houses, and even churches. Something or someone brings us satisfaction for a while, but it just doesn't last, so we need something new. In that mindset we can't see that an idol, even an upgraded one, will never satisfy. It's a bottomless pit of diminishing returns.

Bouncing from one thing to another for only a short-term buzz should tip us off to the insufficiency of our idols. But we are sometimes like the idol builder who can't see what's going on.

> No one considers, nor is there knowledge or discernment to say, "Half of it I burned in the fire; I also baked bread on its coals; I roasted meat and have eaten. And shall I make the rest of it an abomination? Shall I fall down before a block of wood?" He feeds on ashes; a deluded heart has led him astray, and he cannot deliver himself or say, "Is there not a lie in my right hand?"
>
> (Isaiah 44:19–20)

Sometimes our hearts are so hard and our senses so dull that we can't see the absurdity of the idols we hold.

THE ZOO

During one of my lulls in pastoral ministry, I started to branch out and see what else I could do with my life. (By the way, your pastor probably does this more than you think.) I know it's semi-blasphemous to say, but sometimes being a pastor is boring. The pushback is always to ask questions. Are you having a daily time with the Lord in the Word and prayer? Yep. Are you looking at porn or involved in something elicit? Nope. Are you studying and creating fresh sermons? Yep. Are you evangelizing? Yep. Are you in an accountable community? Yep. I was doing my duty, but I was bored. So, I explored and inquired about new opportunities.

I seriously considered becoming a policeman because that sounded exciting. Buying and selling real estate was another option on the table that seemed kind of cool. I also explored joining a variety of non-profits in education and child welfare that were on the cutting edge. But the most adventurous opportunity I considered was buying a zoo. No joke! There was this run-down old zoo that was being sold. Don't think a zoo with "lions and tigers and bears, oh my!" But more along the lines of diseased peacocks, neglected camels, and deranged donkeys. This was a zoo from the *Twilight Zone*, and I wanted it to be mine.

Ask the question: How can a pastor with countless years of biblical schooling, two decades in ministry shepherding a great and supportive congregation consider sabotaging his calling in order to buy a creepy zoo? That makes about as much sense as a guy taking the same piece of wood and using it for heat, food, and worship. Absurd!

THE GREAT EXCHANGE

In order to get the clearest picture possible of my zookeeper heart, you need to see idolatry in terms of the great exchange. Romans 1:23 says that humans "exchanged the glory of the immortal God for images resembling mortal man and birds and animals and reptiles." In the great exchange, humans chose not to give glory to God but to stoop to worship some form of the creation. For me, I wasn't bowing down and worshipping animals, but I was bowing down to the novelty and adventure that the animals provided. God and what

He chose to provide was not enough, so I went in search of my own satisfaction in something exotic. It's like the heart's default is always on the lookout for the next great exchange and to worship anything else besides God.

Some years ago, my twelve-year-old son had his tonsils and adenoids (he referred to them as "androids") removed. The poor boy was in extreme pain and would go into fits of hysterical screaming and out-of-control wailing. When this would happen at night, my wife would try to lie down with him and calm him down. She was doing the best she could, but it would take forever for him to fall back to sleep. My wife was willing to do it over and over again until I came up with a better idea. The next time he woke up in a hysterical fit, I stuck an iPad in his face. My son has always loved the iPad, and the iPad was the overnight fix. He'd wake up, start to get hysterical, play the iPad, and then go back to sleep. So, for the next few nights he substituted an iPad in place of his mom. The great exchange had taken place! Instead of a loving, kind, and caring mom calming him down to go back to sleep, he exchanged her for an iPad.

I'm not dogging on my boy but I'm trying to make a point at his expense: All of our hearts are prone to the great exchange. It's as though we say, "God, You are not worthy of our honor and praise, so we are turning instead to idols." God's not enough, so we search for a suitable replacement. God's not coming through as we had hoped, so it's time to build something better on our own terms. It's *me* time!

I *need* sexual satisfaction, so I will go and get it any way I want. I *need* comfort, so I will find it in food, drink, or drugs. I *need* fun, so I will go on an exciting vacation or adventurous cruise. I *need* security, so I will find it in my salary and my retirement account. I *need* control, so I will force it through anger or manipulation.

Rather than letting God tell us what we need and finding it in Him, we determine what we need and go in search of the idol to fulfill it. More precisely, we don't just search for an idol to fulfill it; we create that very idol.

To put it bluntly: I'm not primarily worshipping the idol but *me*. Who is playing God in idol worship? Me. Who is ultimately playing God in creating the trivial life? Me. Your idol alone holds no power in itself but in the fact that you created it to satisfy when ultimately only God can satisfy. This is important because when you repent of idol worship, you not only repent of your worship of the idol but, more importantly, your creation of it as well.

REPENT AND REBUILD

The good news is that Jesus died for idolaters like you and me. Whether you have been immersed in building a long-term trivial project or a short-term mini idol, you can repent and start fresh. God has a consistent pattern of grace and patience with His idolatrous people. He doesn't scrap them and start over but restores and renews them so they can worship Him alone. And He does this in such a way that you are not crushed by your sin but overwhelmed by His grace.

That's why it's helpful to repent in specifics rather than generalities. You see the surface sin, but what's below the surface sin? What's the idol below the idol? You can call a *BIG* house an idol all day long, but the heart idol could be wanting comfort, security, or recognition for having "made it." Recognition, comfort, and security are not bad things in and of themselves. But when these good things are elevated as ultimate things, one exchanges the recognition, comfort, and security in God alone for the trivial idol of a *BIG* house.

I find it extremely humbling to repent in detail before the Lord. "Father, please forgive me for trying to buy a zoo for the purposes of adventure, fulfillment, happiness, and escape from the mundane necessity of daily faithfulness. I have all I need in Christ, but I'm quick to exchange it for such foolishness." As embarrassing as those specifics may be, it's stunning to know that Jesus didn't just die for my sins in general but in detail. He knew all my gory junk, and still went to the cross in my place to bear the wrath of God. And He pulled off an even greater exchange by taking on my sin and giving me His perfect righteousness. Unbelievable!

The flipside of repentance in detail is grace in detail. Not only can you repent of visioneering in specifics, but you can find the distinct parts of grace in the rebuilding. Your heart can move forward, visioneering on the particulars of God's grace in Jesus Christ. The benefits of Christ are yours in abundance:

○ In Christ, you have love and the search is over.
○ In Christ, you have forgiveness and need not jump through hoops.

- In Christ, you have abundance and lack no good thing.
- In Christ, you have adoption and are never without a Father.
- In Christ, you have security and there's never a breach.
- In Christ, you have acceptance and need not prove a thing.
- In Christ, you have sorrows carried and never buried.
- In Christ, you have a future and your past can't steal it away.

By faith, you can start to visioneer from a heart not only transformed by Jesus but motivated by all the blessings you have in Christ. Just as the gospel lays bare the motives of trivial visioneering, so it also gives hope that there can be something much more fulfilling and weightier. It's a *positive* great exchange where your personal building project is abandoned as Christ takes over to visioneer as He sees fit. And when Christ is the engineer and architect of your life, you never know where you will end up.

Over the years, I have tried to lay before the Lord my visioneering projects. Sometimes my motives trip me up, but God has graciously brought me back on track. It really is a faith adventure to submit to the Lord in life's daily plans, but the rubber meets the road in some of the bigger shifts that require an open heart to go wherever He calls. After graduation from seminary, I moved from Dallas to Los Angeles to serve the Lord among the younger postmodern Generation X. The move required faith, but the call made sense. A few years later He called me to transition to Chicago in order to engage the even younger intellectual millennials, which made sense as well. But the next move was something only God could visioneer, and it seemed a bit out of the zone. After planting me for two decades in the urban areas of Los Angeles and Chicago, God saw fit to move me to the middle of Arkansas where I now minister to the aging Boomers and Builders. I never saw it coming but I see the wisdom in His plan. And in a great twist of providence, I'm in a rural area *and* on a farm. I guess I got my zoo after all!

CHAPTER
3

—— All In ——

H ot Springs Village, Arkansas, is quite the place. A sprawling 26,000 acres makes it the largest gated community in America. Comparisons are few and it's almost impossible to explain what it's like. Imagine trees, golf courses, lakes, mountains, and more trees. People come here from all over to retire. Don't think of the typical retirement community of people driving around town in golf carts or hanging out all day at the city center shopping and drinking coffee. It's more like a forest that has created its own self-contained civilization for people to live out the last third of their life.

It's an amazing place for me to be because I've seen hundreds of young people launch in life, but I usually don't know how they turn out over the long haul. Now, I'm ministering in a retirement community and watching people land in life. They are still visioneering to some extent but the journey on this earth is almost over.

So, how was it? There are the usual mistakes, regrets, and huge misses that go along with the successes, joys and home runs. But most of them will tell me, "I did not see it coming." They never imagined their life turning out the way that it has. The results of the past seventy-plus years have shaped who they are today. But life's not over. Ask them how they are doing, and they will say things like: "It's a good day to be above ground," or "It's a great day to be seen and not viewed." They didn't come here to die but to live.

LAUNCHING AND LANDING

In a conversation with my daughter's fifteen-year-old friend, she was telling us where she wanted to go to college, where she planned to live after college, and where she wanted to retire. Who talks like that at fifteen? She's on the front end of launching in life. I'm sure some of the retirees would love to go back and give some advice to their fifteen-year-old selves. But whether we are launching or landing, we're all still visioneering our lives and eventually the results will be evident to all.

Such was the case for one of the greatest and wisest men to have ever lived, King Solomon. His launch was a heralded success, but his landing was a historic crash. He came to the throne following his father, King David, who was a man after God's own heart. One night in a dream the Lord appeared to King Solomon and said, "Ask for whatever you want me to give you." (1 Kings 3:5 NIV). Solomon didn't ask for riches or that his enemies be conquered, but he asked for wisdom. God answered by gifting Solomon with the ability to know and dispense wisdom. The book of Proverbs contains many of his wise sayings that were intended to instruct those launching in life. It's as though he takes the young person by the hand and warns him about rushing unreflectively through life. Instead, he promotes a life of wisdom and God-given competence to navigate through the details of life for the glory of God. Solomon was the master instructor in the weighty life.

But many years later we meet up with the aging Solomon who has clearly gone off the rails. As he reflects on his life in the book of Ecclesiastes, we see that his launching does not match his landing. There seems to be a disconnect between his own teaching and living. Proverbs contains his instruction challenging normal behaviors, thinking patterns, and motives, while Ecclesiastes reveals that he failed to preach to himself but instead went along with the default mode of the human heart. His orthodoxy was solid while his orthopraxy was skewed. His doctrine aimed at the weighty life, but his practice pursued the trivial life.

Solomon went *all in* on the trivial life. He took his wisdom, wealth, power, and passions, and pursued the trivial life to the extent that no human had ever done or ever will do. And when he finally reflected on his landing, his conclusion was along the lines of "What was I doing?" At the end of his life, he saw all the futility in the many ways that he turned from God. Rather than aligning with the kingdom of God, he aligned with the kingdom of darkness. Ecclesiastes is his story of repentance. You may not have the wisdom, wealth, power, and passions to build the trivial life to the extent of Solomon; nevertheless, you can still be all in. Trivial pursuits may not be your stated intention or aim, but your launching and landing can be tainted nonetheless. What are you doing?

ALL IN AND ALL OUT

Imagine having all the money in the world at your disposal, and all the power and authority to do whatever you want. What would you do? Solomon had it all, plus the bonus of wisdom, and went all in and all out pursuing the trivial life. He's not throwing shade, but he's speaking the truth when he says, "I have acquired great wisdom, surpassing all who were over Jerusalem before me, and my heart has had great experience of wisdom and knowledge" (Ecclesiastes 1:16). If anyone had the wisdom and resources to make life work for ultimate meaning, it was Solomon.

He tried to cheer himself with alcohol in order to see if it was something worthwhile to do in the few days he had here on this earth. The stash of cash was overflowing with silver and gold to acquire the best singers and musicians to entertain his soul. And, of course, his life was filled with lots and lots of women. What more could a man of the world want? He had money, good music, lots of sex, and fame. How much money did he have? More than you can imagine. How good was the music? Pick any singer or group you like, and Solomon could have them playing in his backyard. Sex life? More than a thousand women. Greatness? The greatest to have ever lived. Solomon had more pleasure than you will ever have because he went to the extreme in making himself happy and satisfied.

Solomon was also bursting with achievements and accomplishments. Dream homes were built at his command. This guy created exquisite vineyards, gardens, and parks. Reservoirs were constructed to water his forest of growing trees. Herds and flocks under his possession far outnumbered the holdings of anyone ever in Jerusalem. The slaves he acquired for labor were part of his possession for so long that the slaves started giving birth to future slaves. And the way that Solomon tells the story is that the entirety of these possessions and achievements were all for himself. This was not for the benefit of the community but all for himself because he was all in and went all out pursuing the trivial life.

Now this is the part where you think I'm going to tell you that he didn't like all that music, women, money, and achievements. Oh no, he liked it all! "And whatever my eyes desired I did not keep from them. I kept my heart from no pleasure, for my heart found pleasure in all my toil, and this was my reward for all my toil" (Ecclesiastes 2:10). He enjoyed it all, and pleasure was his reward!

POINTLESS VAPOR

Something seems awfully familiar in all of his pursuits. Does it remind you of anyone? He built gardens with lots of trees and watering systems. Sound familiar? He acquired people and animals. Sound familiar? Solomon is trying to play God. The world's messed up, but he thinks he can fix it and put it back together as it was in the beginning. Eden didn't work out so well, so let's have a do-over. Solomon is his own little sovereign who feels the fractured world and sets out to "reverse the curse," so to speak. The earthly king separated himself from the true King in order to find meaning. It didn't work for Solomon, and it won't work for you.

Upon further reflection on all he had done, he concludes that his pursuits turned up empty and trivial. "Then I considered all that my hands had done and the toil I had expended in doing it, and behold, all was vanity and a striving after wind, and there was nothing to be gained under the sun" (Ecclesiastes 2:11). The word Solomon often returns to is *vanity*, which basically means *pointless vapor*. Life seems pointless, so what do you actually gain after all the hard work and frenzied activity? Nothing. In addition, life is short-lived like a vapor, and then comes death. Though Solomon was all in pursuing meaning and happiness in life, it was just a chasing after the wind—he caught nothing. Death would still come for him, and he would be left with no lasting gain under the sun.

So what? He had fun while it lasted. He had lots of money, sex, music, wisdom, and accomplishments. Who cares if there is nothing left when it is all said and done? This pushback overlooks two significant realities. First, no matter how much you have, you will always want more. It's the pointless cycle of "Enough is never enough." Second, you can chase after the wind all you want here on this earth, but you won't catch anything, and your trivial pursuits will soon come to an abrupt end in your death.

When I was thirty-three, I received a Christmas card from a woman named Iris. She used to help me out at a nursing home where I preached while I was in seminary. This was the second largest nursing home in Dallas, Texas. I loved the residents and they loved me. I'm not going to lie; I was pretty famous in that nursing home. As Solomon was famous in Israel, so I was famous in that nursing home. Iris updated me on how things were going at the nursing home and how the new preacher was getting along. Then she wrote one sentence that basically said, "There is no one here who remembers you." Humbled and cut down a bit, I wanted to ask, "What do you mean, no one remembers me? I used to know over a hundred residents! That is where I began my preaching and ministering. I loved them and they loved me." There was no one there who knew me because they were all dead. So much for my earthly legacy. I was thirty-three years old and already *not* leaving an earthly legacy. I feel you, Solomon. I feel you.

GREATER THAN SOLOMON

A friend and I were in Las Vegas for a church conference at the same time as the International Consumer Electronics Show, where a lot of innovative technology is introduced. Bill Gates, Microsoft's founder, was speaking at the show and his computer froze up during his presentation. Let that sink in. That's what Solomon felt and that's what he wants us to feel—not the thought that we are so innovative and creative, and we're going to make a name for ourselves that's going to last. But like a frozen computer, the pursuits in this life are getting us nowhere. We are not making traction, and are ultimately accomplishing nothing of lasting value. There is no gain in trivial pursuits!

Please understand that there is nothing wrong in wanting to achieve and accomplish great things or to be happy and pursue a life of meaning. What's wrong is pursuing this on your own terms as a little god trying to restore paradise. You would never say that you are trying to return to Eden or restore paradise. That would be weird. But that's your heart's default mode. You are internally wired to construct a life of meaning and happiness on your own visioneering terms. But if Solomon has taught us anything, it's that all human attempts to find gain, meaning, and satisfaction outside of God will ultimately end in futility. There is no returning to the Garden, no matter how ambitious the efforts.

But God has made a way of return. Someone greater than Solomon has come on the scene (Matthew 12:42). In the arrival of Jesus Christ, we see One who not only embodied the wisdom of God in His teaching but actually followed through perfectly in His obedience. Solomon failed; Jesus did not. And now the way to an Edenlike existence has been made known through Jesus Christ. We don't need to create it but simply live in it by faith. At the moment, it's not an actual garden, as that comes later (Revelation 22:1–2), but the fellowship with God is just as real. We are no longer cast out of the Father's presence but walk with Him in the cool of the day (Genesis 3:8). The relationship that was in the Garden has now been restored through Jesus Christ.

The One greater than Solomon not only helps us make sense of this life, but He also gives us meaning beyond death.

Our desires, words, and actions in real time are not wasted but can extend into eternity for the glory of God. This means that we can be *all in* and go *all out* for the weighty life. None of it will be wasted! The One greater than Solomon gives us meaning, purpose, and gain in this life and the life to come.

A Minor Issue

I hate to rain on this glorious parade, but a minor issue needs to be acknowledged. The dominant view throughout history is that King Solomon wrote the book of Ecclesiastes. The thought is that at the end of his life Solomon saw all the futility in the many ways that he had turned from God. It's his story of repentance. However, it must be acknowledged that we have no historical record of Solomon turning back to God *besides* what is seen in the book of Ecclesiastes. When you check in on his life in Kings 11, he is married to a variety of pagan women and worshipping their gods.

Another view that seems to be more prominent among scholars today is that this is not Solomon but someone pretending to be Solomon as a literary device. You could call it Solomonic—not in a deceptive way but in a way that gets the point of the book across using a literary device that was known at the time. The author takes on the persona of Solomon in order to present wisdom from someone such as Solomon who explored a variety of areas in life to acquire meaning but was left empty.

Back and forth it's debated, not just if Solomon wrote Ecclesiastes but whether or not he repented. I could give a lot of textual arguments from Ecclesiastes on why I think Solomon is the author. My heart hopes he wrote it because I want things to have ended well for the second wisest person to ever live. I want Solomon to have landed in a state of repentance, turning away from other gods and having the godly perspective presented in the book of Ecclesiastes.

Why bring this up now? Because this minor issue is actually quite major when you focus on your own life. Think about it: the second wisest person to have ever lived strayed from the Lord and may have never returned. Full-blown idolatry and triviality may have consumed him to the end. If the second wisest person to have ever lived strayed from the Lord, then what hope is there for you and me to not do the same? That's a scary question. The next chapter will point to the way of escape from the trivial life for good. But for now, pay attention to your launching and landing. In fact, forget your launch and press on toward your permanent landing. Most of us can't go back and redo our launch, but we can pay attention to how we land. Your launch in life may have been solid, but don't make your landing a crash. In the end, you *can* stick the landing.

STICK THE LANDING

As I spend my days interacting with the retirement community in the middle of Arkansas, I hear echoes of Solomon's life. I've seen none of them launch in life, but their stories reveal that some were all in for the trivial life. Excitement gripped them in the prime of their lives as they followed Solomon down the road of accomplishments and achievements, but it was often at the cost of their family and integrity. Others bounced from one relationship to the next, and their convoluted family histories would even give Solomon a run for his money.

But I get to hear their stories in testimony form of repentance and faith in the One greater than Solomon. They have found forgiveness and mercy in Jesus Christ. Unlike Solomon, their repentance is not debatable because they are humble and broken for all to see and give glory to God alone. And though the trivial life may have once ruled the day, they now are all in and going all out for the weighty life. They plan to stick the landing.

You should have hope that no matter how miserably you have botched your launch, you can still land for the glory of God. A renewed life means a rerouted trajectory. The trivial life may be your backstory, but it doesn't have to be your narrative moving forward. One greater than Solomon has a habit of redeeming trivial lives and transforming them into weighty lives that stick the landing.

CHAPTER
4

——— Escape ———

After I became a Christian at age nineteen, a number of former sins dropped out of my life completely, such as cursing, stealing, and speeding. Okay, maybe not speeding altogether, but a lot of sins really did go away for good. Sexual immorality, however, seemed to have an unbreakable death grip on me. Bondage that seemed inescapable came in the form of what I call the "3 Ss." The *sex* part was with others, the *skin* part was with pornography, and the *self-abuse* part was with myself. These three were my reality before conversion, and seemed impossible to escape.

One by one, over the course of two years, they fell away. The first S dropped off as I not only personally repented but also asked others for forgiveness. Through personal meetings and phone calls, I asked a variety of girls to forgive me. Some received it well with appreciation, while others thought there was nothing to apologize for—but, either way, it was part of my journey to freedom.

The other two Ss were still hanging around. At first, I didn't think it was a big deal because I wasn't bothering anyone. Over the summer when I was twenty, I served as a youth intern at a church. Once, I had to stay overnight in a hotel before working the next day on a Sunday. On Saturday night I was watching something inappropriate in the hotel. The next day I was up front leading the church in the Lord's Prayer, and I fumbled and mumbled as I was plagued with mass conviction. The second S had to go.

The last S tended to be the most stubborn, being locked into my own immoral thoughts with the goal of fulfillment in myself. But God broke me with the thought, *Are you going to please Me or keep pleasing yourself?* Rather than focusing on myself during temptation, the focus shifted to God alone.

This testimony to my freedom is far more embarrassing for me to write than for you to read. The purpose is to demonstrate that what once felt like an impossibility to escape became a new reality of freedom. Please don't get the impression that I no longer struggle with lust. The fight with my eyes and the battle within my heart are real. But, by God's grace, I am no longer in bondage to the 3 Ss but have escaped into real freedom.

Have you ever felt in bondage to a sin with no possibility of escape—that no matter what you did, that sin would do you in and hold you captive the rest of your life? Maybe you are in that sin right now. Hopelessness can be debilitating. Shame feels overwhelming. But if I'm reading Scripture correctly, and I think I am, you need to know that you can have real freedom—deliverance from not only that particular sin, but also freedom from the trivial life that tends to manifest itself in a variety of sins. Not make-believe freedom but real freedom in the here and now.

THE WAY OF ESCAPE

My office has a wonderful black leather couch that was bought off of Craigslist many years ago. It's such a comfy couch. When I'm not studying on the couch or taking nap breaks, the couch has a lot of stories to tell. It's the counseling couch. Though I'm bound to confidentiality, the couch is not. The couch has heard confessions of sin that range from adultery and addiction all the way to abuse and abandonment. Individuals can be manageable while couples can be downright nasty. Some of the language they hurl at each other would receive an R rating. This is all in the presence of a pastor, so I can't imagine what they say while alone. Through all the broken stories, tears, fears, and hopelessness, there seems to always be a common theme, "I'm trapped. There is no way of escape." But the bleakness felt on the black leather couch doesn't have to be the end of the story.

One of my favorite *escape* verses is 1 Corinthians 10:13: "No temptation has overtaken you that is not common to man. God is faithful, and he will not let you be tempted beyond your ability, but with the temptation he will also provide the way of escape, that you may be able to endure it." The passage is pretty straightforward. No matter the temptation you are facing, it's not abnormal or unique to you alone. Common temptations and sins, such as immorality, greed, jealousy, anger, etc., plague humanity.

You are neither the first person to feel these temptations nor will you be the last. Temptations are a normal part of life, even the Christian life. But you will never come to a point where you have to give in, because God has set a limit on the temptation. You are never going to get boxed in where you have to fall into sin. The way of escape will always be there for you to take so that you can endure the temptation without giving in.

The context of the verse is smack dab in the middle of the trivial life. Paul has been encouraging the Corinthians to press on in their faith, and then he switches to warn them against idolatry. He proceeds to tell them a story of the ancient Israelites who had all the blessings of God in abundance, yet they went down the road of the trivial life.

While in the desert and being nourished by God, the Israelites still turned aside to all forms of foolishness. Even though they had experienced the miraculous deliverance out of Egypt and the mighty guidance of God ever since, they still went their own way. Paul recaps Israel's history for our benefit as he says, "Now these things happened as examples for us, so that we would not crave evil things as they also craved" (1 Corinthians 10:6, NASB). Don't go down the same road of foolishness and triviality! Some sought satisfaction in sexual immorality and 23,000 were killed in one day (1 Corinthians 10:7–8). Others who questioned the provision and grace of God were subsequently killed by snakes (1 Corinthians 10:9). Still others complained against the leadership, and the destroying angel took them out (1 Corinthians 10:10).

All of these scenarios were examples and warnings for our benefit (1 Corinthians 10:11). Even though we can have all the salvation blessings of the Lord, we can still default to the trivial life. Watch out! There must be an intentional effort to stand firm in the Lord (1 Corinthians 10:12). Most in the desert failed to take the way of escape, but there can be a different outcome for you. No sin has to take you out as there will always be a way out. The trivial life may be tempting but God promises the way of escape. Take it!

RENEWAL OF THE MIND

Practically speaking, the way of escape can be found in the "put off" and "put on" language of the Bible. It's a taking off the trivial life and putting on the weighty life. The context of this teaching is Paul's instruction to the Ephesians to no longer live like unbelievers "in the futility of their minds" (Ephesians 4:17). One of the issues from their past was skewed and flawed thinking patterns. Dark thoughts often led down the road of processing life, in line with emptiness and triviality.

Many of these thought patterns that were laid down before you were saved have developed deep ruts and you can still get stuck. Years of dark thinking can still be the default today. How can you escape the trivial life in your thinking? By continual renewal and reformation of the mind. Paul encourages you to put off the old corrupt and deceitful patterns and to "be renewed in the spirit of your minds" (Ephesians 4:23). In the past, your mind was steeped in futility, but in the present your mind can be renewed and transformed. "Do not be conformed to this world, but be transformed by the renewal of your mind, that by testing you may discern what is the will of God, what is good and acceptable and perfect" (Romans 12:2).

God is in the process of changing your thought patterns to be more like His thought patterns. But you are not inactive in the process. You can use God-given means toward the goal of being renewed in the spirit of your mind. That is, you can intentionally do things that can influence your thinking toward God and His ways. It's natural to think about what you put in front of you. If you put sports in front of you, then you will think about sports. If you put social media before you, then you will think about your feed. But if you put God's Word in front of you, then you will think about God and His priorities. You think about what you put before you.

Several years ago, I was at one of my lowest points in life. In fact, I was so low I didn't even want to live anymore but just leave this earth altogether. I had a lot of scary thoughts. I went to see a very wise, older man who helped me think through a lot of issues that were going on in my life and in my heart. He offered me much healing grace through Jesus Christ. One of the tools he gave me to get my thinking back on track was Scripture memory. He said I needed to replace my messed-up thinking with the Word of God. Thus began a pattern of Scripture memory that developed out of a sense of desperation to think God's thoughts after Him. It's not a brag or even a humblebrag, but I have memorized hundreds of verses and even books of the Bible. It reveals my desperation to escape the thinking pattern of the trivial life, and to think God's thoughts after Him in the weighty life.

The amount of time you spend in God's Word reveals the amount of your desperation—not necessarily a suicidal desperation but a realization that the world is out to shape you. Your past ways of thinking will shape you by default if you are not intentionally being shaped by God's Word. You need to come to a point of desperation where you can't live another day unless your thinking is saturated by God and His Word.

PUT OFF, PUT ON

It's in this context of transformed thinking that you can now put off the trivial life and put on the weighty life. Paul says "to put off your old self, which belongs to your former manner of life and is corrupt through deceitful desires, and to be renewed in the spirit of your minds, and to put on the new self, created after the likeness of God in true righteousness and holiness" (Ephesians 4:22–24). Paul is describing what has already happened to believers. In Christ, the old self was put off and the new self was put on. Now you are to live in this new reality of holiness by putting off and putting on in your daily experience.

○ Put off lying—Put on speaking the truth (Ephesians 4:25).

○ Put off impurity—Put on holiness and purity (Ephesians 4:19, 24).

○ Put off greed—Put on generosity (Ephesians 4:19, 28).

○ Put off anger—Put on humility and patience (Colossians 3:8, 12).

○ Put off harshness—Put on gentleness and compassion (Colossians 3:8, 12).

○ Put off stealing—Put on productive work (Ephesians 4:28).

○ Put off words that tear down—Put on words that build up (Ephesians 4:29).

○ Put off bitterness—Put on forgiveness (Ephesians 4:31–32).

○ Put off hatred—Put on love (Colossians 3:8, 14).

The downfall of many efforts to escape is the failure to "put on." The Christian life is more than just fighting sin. If you kick out one sin, you need to put on righteousness in its place or another sin will just sneak back in. It's a strange phenomenon that one idol can be dislodged only to make room for another idol. A man kicks out lust and replaces it with obsessive exercise. A woman kicks out materialism and replaces it with compulsive minimalism. Some swaps don't seem to be as destructive, but they are still a distraction from wholehearted devotion.

Walking with the Lord is not just about escaping the trivial life but also leaning into the weighty life. The Bible is not a rule book telling you what not to do. It's actually a word of grace turning you away from those things that lead to destruction and turning you toward those things that lead to life. That's why you can't just focus on the "put off" verses but must also focus on the "put on" replacements. It's not just about escaping the trivial life but living in the fullness of the weighty life.

COMMUNITY

I don't like the entertainment of escape rooms. These rooms—so much like a large puzzle—offer clues and tips on how to go through a process of escape. Participants rummage through the room looking for a way out before the clock runs out and they are locked in. They are intended for fun, but I see them as maddening. That's why I rely on others to help get me out. I never get the riddles, nor can I figure out the math codes. I'm clueless and I completely lean on others to figure it out. If I were left on my own, I would never escape.

Similarly, I feel the same way navigating life on my own. The Word of God can be transforming my mind and I can be in full "put off" and "put on" mode, but, left to myself, I become easily distracted and discouraged. Perhaps you feel the same way. You and I need the community of the Body of Christ to help us escape the trivial life and live in the fullness of the weighty life. Encouragement and exhortation are both needed during the launching years, landing years and everything in between. I'm not sure if different forms of encouragement and exhortation are needed at each phase of life, but it sure feels like it.

After I became a Christian, I didn't know how to date or to treat girls in a godly way. So, relationships went off my radar for several years. In addition, my parents got a divorce, which made me afraid of marriage. I was searching for something radical and I found it in a book called *Dating with Integrity*. Here is the gist: Don't go out on a date with a girl, because if you don't like the girl or you break up, that would be hurting your sister in Christ. Instead, go out in groups of friends and serve in groups of friends. If you see a girl you like, then talk to her in a group and get to know her in a group. Then after talking to her and getting to know her in a group, ask her to marry you. And that's what I did.

My wife and I knew each other at fifteen years of age but did not date in high school. She became a follower of Christ, and I did as well at age nineteen in a different state. We kept in casual contact over the years. Fast forward to when I was twenty-five years old.

I was in my last year of seminary, and my future wife served in the college group that I led. In addition, she helped me in a nursing-home ministry from time to time. We talked, but it would be a big stretch to say that we were dating. After talking to her friends and my friends, without talking to her, I decided to ask her to marry me. I went to ask her parents' permission and her mom said, "What does my daughter think about this?" I said, "I don't know, I've never talked to her about it." We never had any such conversation about "I like you," and "You like me," and such. None.

The next day, I asked her to pack her bags and go on a road trip with me from Texas to Arkansas to my parents' house. Over the next five hours in the car ride, we listened to cassette tapes that I created for the occasion. On the tapes I was reading parts of my journal about my life and perhaps her involvement with it. Interspersed with the reading were worship songs (not sung by me). Yes, for five hours she listened to me reading and worship songs. The last entry of my journal that I read on the tape said, "I love her and I'm going to ask her to marry me." I pulled off the highway and we just happened to be in Gum Springs, Arkansas, population 113. We went back in the woods and I asked her to marry me. And she said . . . "Yes."

Please do not follow my example. I went so overboard in trying to avoid the trivial life that I entered the dorky life. My poor wife! There is a much better way to proceed with godly dating and engagement. The reason why I tell this story is because of the community that walked with me during the process. The wisdom given to me was to be cautious and bold. I would meet with my peers to discuss what I looked for in a future wife, and they would urge me to be cautious because marriage was a lifelong commitment. Other interactions were with those older than me, such as my teachers and pastors. They saw my fear and encouraged me to be bold.

Caution and boldness are a great combo of wisdom to those launching in life. Younger people can be timid and need others to speak into their lives to go for it (2 Timothy 1:7). At the same time, proceeding with caution often comes from those who have walked the path before us. The older generation can see the trivial landmines and reroute you toward the weighty life. If you are young, you may have the energy to go all out for the Lord but do it around faithful brothers and sisters who can run with you.

Midlife tends to bring another set of challenges combining raising kids, caring for aging adults, and all the drama in between. Many go off the rails in search of excitement and a break from the mundane. Whether it's my desire for a zoo or your desire to abdicate responsibilities and relationships, midlife can be tricky. All stages of life are prone to self-deception, but midlife carries some unique traps. Left alone we can easily be self-deceived.

John DuPont, who is portrayed in the movie *Foxcatcher*, was a self-deceived man. Extremely wealthy and having an interest in wrestling, he invested in training the US Olympic men's team and even had his own private training facility. He viewed himself as a coach of sorts with a lot of gifts and abilities. But he just surrounded himself with others who played into his self-deception and jealousies. They were basically paid to praise and adore him. DuPont even surrounded himself with trivial trophies and fake accomplishments. But he cracked under his jealousies, which eventually led him to murder a member of the wrestling team. When the movie was over, I heard someone in the theater say, "That was disturbing."

There is something disturbing when we see others self-deceived and self-destructive. It's easy to see the self-deception in people like John DuPont, but not as easy in ourselves. We are all prone to self-deception but especially during midlife. The temptation is to highlight our accomplishments while hiding our failures, to project the image of having it all together even if we are deeply disturbed within. I've seen men and women put on airs of invincibility as they headed for the cliff of self-destruction. Often there is a mismatch between what they say and what they actually do. They can even give props to the weighty life while being all in for the trivial life. Those in midlife desperately need the Body of Christ to escape from their own elaborate room of self-deception.

Christ-centeredness and authentic community provide a pathway to freedom. Those in your sphere of fellowship must both point you to Jesus while promoting an atmosphere of honesty and authenticity. On the one hand, you want to pray, "Search me, O God, and know my heart" (Psalm 39:23); while on the other, it seems wise to invite others in and say, "Search me and tell me what you see." Of course, we do this in all phases of life, but it's especially needed in midlife. There is something inside of us that feels like we should have it together by now, and we really don't want to acknowledge that something is off. That's why it's so key for believers to promote a safe place for others to be honest and authentic without the threat of judgment or abandonment. Grace and understanding must abound for others to escape and walk in the light of life.

The back end of landing in life can be filled with joy but also great suffering. The show *60 Minutes* once followed a couple for ten years from diagnosis to the final stages of Alzheimer's. Carol was diagnosed in 2008, and her husband, Mike, was her caregiver. Each year, *60 Minutes* interviewed them to show the devastating impact of Alzheimer's. Carol deteriorated to where she didn't even know her husband's name, then she didn't know her own name, and finally she got to the point where she couldn't even talk. It was very emotional, especially as you see the decline of her husband, who was a former New York City cop. You feel for him as he goes through bouts of depression and even becomes suicidal. As his wife no longer speaks and barely moves, he says that he feels that "Carol's gone."

What in the world do you say? Situations similar to these have come my way as I serve a church of senior citizens. Some of the scenarios are heartbreaking and soul crushing. But people need not be alone. The church community is strong and offers tremendous support. They themselves know what it's like to land and face difficulties during the last phase of life.

The needed exhortation is to press on, and the specific encouragement is to press in. It's time to keep going until you are with the Lord. Until you see Him face to face, you need to stay focused to finish strong. Life can be discouraging and can lead to doubt and cynicism, but now is not the time to quit. Press on. At the same time, there are fellow travelers just like you who are walking the road marked with suffering. Get to know them and their stories. Press in. Take the time to both give and receive encouragement as you press on and press into community.

No matter what phase of life you find yourself in, you need the Body of Christ. The temptation during challenges and trials will be to run and hide. Don't bail out. Fight against this default mode, and lean into community. God has provided specific people for your exhortation and encouragement.

There's no way you can make it on your own, and you're not supposed to. The God who saved you is the same One who placed you into His family for your flourishing. The church is part of God's grand plan to help you escape the trivial life and walk in the fullness of the weighty life.

REAL FREEDOM

Escape may feel impossible because you are in too deep. The trivial life is all-consuming, and you can't see a way out. I'm with you. I've been there several times. But you need to know that there is always grace to escape. Your situation may seem complicated but your path to real freedom isn't. Too many times we distort and complicate what one must do to walk with God.

It's like all the remotes that are needed to turn on my TV. It's amazing how complicated we've made these systems. Our TV takes three remotes to work. It's an old TV that the previous owners left imbedded in the fireplace never to be removed. The TV itself does not have its own remote. You can use an old DirecTV remote to turn on the power, but it will give you no signal. Next, you need the new DirecTV remote to turn on the DirecTV console to get a signal to the TV. If you push the wrong buttons, you will mess up the inputs and you will be lost forever. After you have done these two actions successfully, you might have a picture but still no sound. There's a separate system for volume that has its own complicated remote. So, if you ever come over to my house, you will be able to take all three remotes and figure out my TV. Confused?

Maybe you feel just as confused right now about your way of escape—that you have to jump through all types of hoops and do it just right and then hopefully it will work. But the way of escape is simple, not complicated. It's a matter of repentance and faith in Jesus, followed by a consistent path of growth. Get into the Word and let the Word get into you. Put off your former way of life and put on the newness you have in Christ. Find a church where you are fully known and fully loved. And just know, in the midst of all your struggles and temptations, there will always be a way of escape. Take it!

CHAPTER
5

Elements

Demolition is a fun process to watch on TV, as many home make over shows take a room back to its bones before making it over. When the demolition is in your own home, however, that can be another matter altogether, but interesting nonetheless.

Several years ago, we had the kitchen floor replaced in our 1954 Chicago house, and the renovation was more extensive than I had imagined. Just roll a new floor on top of the current one and we'll be good to go. Nope. In clearing the way for the new floor, they had to rip out the current floor, which turned into ripping out four floors. Through the years, the occupants of the house had become dissatisfied with the outdated floor and plopped a new one right on top, four times. Now it was our turn, and we were going to do it *right* by ripping out all the floors and laying a brand-new floor that would last on into eternity.

Ripping out all the four floors was like a journey back in time. The first one was laid when the house was built in the '50s. It's a retro floor that the builders probably thought was *keen*. It was probably not replaced until the late '60s or early '70s with a floor that looks like a sparkly disco ball, which the owners thought was *groovy*. Then again it was replaced in the '80s with a bright yellow patterned floor that was *awesome*. Then probably in the '90s they went with a floor that was quite *rad*. But no matter how perfect the floor the builders put in, it was violently ripped up and thrown away in pieces.

There is something about remodeling that just feels good. Those in the past had bad taste, and we are finally going to get it right. But the layer upon layer of flooring demonstrated that the cycle will continue. Down the road, to my chagrin, our floor will likely be ripped up and tossed aside. No matter how cool we thought our new floor was, one day it will be destroyed.

Over the last several chapters, layer by layer, we have been dismantling the trivial life. The actions and attitudes above the surface were ripped up to show something out of whack below. An inside-out renovation exposed a deceitful heart. But now, in the gospel, there is a new heart with new desires to obey and follow Jesus Christ. An inside-out renovation uncovered idolatry and misplaced worship. But in the gospel, we see all the blessings we have in Christ as He alone is worthy of all our worship. An inside-out renovation brought to light the many ways we seek for meaning, purpose, and gain apart from God. But in the gospel, we have enduring meaning, purpose, and gain through a restored relationship with the Father. An inside-out renovation revealed a fear that there may never be an escape from the trivial life. But in the gospel, there is freedom not only in the world to come but also hope in the here and now.

As the layers of our lives are ripped off, they not only expose the trivial elements that have been in play but also give hope that, through the gospel, a new way of living can take hold. Going forward, you can build in such a way that the outcome is permanence rather than demolition. Though you may have operated in the default mode for quite some time, you can actually head in a different direction. The trivial life can be set aside, and the weighty life can be ushered in.

Two Builders

Jesus once told a story about two builders who achieved two different results. In fact, it was his concluding illustration to his most famous sermon, popularly referred to as the Sermon on the Mount. This is the way he wrapped it up in Matthew 7:24–27:

> *"Everyone then who hears these words of mine and does them will be like a wise man who built his house on the rock. And the rain fell, and the floods came, and the winds blew and beat on that house, but it did not fall, because it had been founded on the rock. And everyone who hears these words of mine and does not do them will be like a foolish man who built his house on the sand. And the rain fell, and the floods came, and the winds blew and beat against that house, and it fell, and great was the fall of it."*

Two builders, two houses, two foundations, two storms, and two results. The builder who built his house on the solid foundation of rock was pointing to the one who heard Jesus' words in the Sermon on the Mount and actually obeyed them. The storm of God's future judgment came but it stood firm. But the builder who built his house on the sand is the foolish one who heard Jesus' words but did not do them. The judgment of God came, and the trivial life he was building fell with a great crash

Jesus' Sermon on the Mount is one of the clearest pictures possible of what it looks like to live the weighty life. Of course, it also shows the default mode of the human heart in all its triviality. Jesus is like a master heart inspector who exposes the building process. He has the plans for a solid foundation as well as the wisdom to avoid a crash. Of course, it all depends on what you do with what He says. It's all about paying attention to what you are building along the way. Let's take a look at a little slice of this convicting sermon.

BUILDING BLOCKS

Jesus launches into his sermon in Matthew 5–7 with a strong opening. In fact, he won't let up the whole sermon. I've heard it said that it's like when someone sticks out his hand to shake yours but instead punches you in the stomach. It's this punch that begins with the Beatitudes, which are basically a series of blessings. And the One giving the blessing is God Himself as He approves of the one who pleases Him. However, the Beatitudes are not a description of how to get

God's approval; rather, they describe those who already have it. Those living under His Lordship, through the Holy Spirit, have distinct internal qualities that lead to godly actions and obedience. It's these elements and building blocks that are essential for living in the fullness of the weighty life.

—— "Blessed are the poor in spirit, for theirs is the kingdom of heaven." (Matthew 5:3)

Jesus' followers are those who are poor in spirit and completely dependent upon God. They have no resources in themselves to survive, so if God does not come through, then it's all over. It's like the man I once saw in a third-world country lying on the sidewalk, totally naked with nothing. At first I thought to myself, *How did he end up like that?* Then I started to panic a bit for him because I wondered, *What does he do next? Where does he go?* There really were no good options for help.

Spiritually speaking, that's you and me. We have nothing and we must look to God's intervention in Christ as our only hope. This element of spiritual poverty is essential for not only salvation but ongoing growth in the Lord. We are never self-sufficient but always Christ-sufficient. In turn, Jesus says we get the blessing of the "kingdom of heaven" in the reign of Christ both now and forever. His gracious rule over our lives is the display of a weighty life of dependence.

— "Blessed are those who mourn, for they shall be comforted." (Matthew 5:4)

Not only should we mourn over our personal sin but the sinful effects of the world. They should grieve us. We are broken and we live within a broken world. This devastation is laid out in a prayer book called *Operation World*. The book presents in detail the spiritual and physical needs of each nation around the world for prayer. The book's listings are in alphabetical order and here are a few nations under the letter B: Brazil has seven million child laborers and 600,000 young girls involved in prostitution. Botswana has the second highest prevalence of AIDS and 100,000 AIDS orphans. Bahrain has over 90 percent of the population perishing without Christ.

Don't turn away from the suffering and just make mourning all about your personal repentance. It's so much more. Believers should not only look inwardly but grieve outwardly over the effects of sin in the world. In turn, the blessedness of those who mourn is the sure promise that they will be comforted—not only the comfort of forgiveness but also the comfort that God alone gives to the one who engages in the pain of the world.

— "Blessed are the meek, for they shall inherit the earth." (Matthew 5:5)

Meekness is not weakness. Two of the strongest and most humble characters of the Bible are Jesus and Moses. Moses, in his time, was called the meekest man on the face of the earth (Numbers 12:3) and Jesus was gentle and humble in heart (Matthew 11:29). And their meekness and humility were demonstrated in their suffering. The statement about Moses' meekness was made when he was under opposition from those closest to him. And the humility of Jesus is seen throughout His life and suffering as He committed His life totally to the Father. It's so obvious that a key element of those in the kingdom is humility. And when pressure is applied, you want humility to come out.

Jesus says that the meek will inherit the earth. What's the connection between humility and land inheritance? The Jews wanted to take back their land from the Romans by force. But Jesus indicates that the land comes through humility. God is not calling us to grab and fight for our rights in this life but to operate under His reign and control. We are not weak as we fight and stand up for the poor, the oppressed, and the suffering. We are under the rule of the King, and one day we will reign with the King as we inherit the earth.

— "Blessed are those who hunger and thirst for righteousness, for they shall be satisfied." (Matthew 5:6)

The righteousness involved here has to do with obedience to God's will. In the same way that we would physically hunger and thirst for literal food and drink, we should hunger and thirst for doing God's will. Those who pursue God and His will in all forms are satisfied in God. We don't fulfill God's will in a detached way out of duty, but we pursue His will in a fulfilling relationship with Him. When He calls us to purity or to help the poor, it's not with the attitude of

"God says it; I guess I have to do it." It's more like "This is my Father's will for me; I long to do it." The pursuit of God's will is the pursuit of satisfaction in God.

This is often hard to grasp for new believers. At times, Christianity can seem like a long list of dos and don'ts. But seen in the context of a relationship with the Father, it starts to make sense that the Father knows what's best for His children. When you start to grasp that God intends good for you and not harm, His rules and paths can seem sweet and satisfying.

— "Blessed are the merciful, for they shall receive mercy." (Matthew 5:7)

Those who operate in the kingdom have the characteristic of mercy. Why? Because they understand that they are also in need of mercy. You can extend forgiveness to those who have offended you because God has graciously extended the hand of forgiveness to you in Christ. You can show mercy to those afflicted emotionally, spiritually, and physically because God has shown mercy to you. God's heart is merciful; and as we have received mercy, we extend the merciful heart of God to others.

Often you may wonder if God is so merciful, then why doesn't He alleviate suffering in the world? There are many ways you can theologically answer that question, but a good response is to see that you are His hands and feet of mercy on this earth. God uses you to extend His heart of mercy. And we can keep showing mercy because, as God gives it to us, it can spill out onto others. And as you and I continue to realize our need for the mercy of God, we can more readily offer it to others.

— "Blessed are the pure in heart, for they shall see God." (Matthew 5:8)

The context shows that the religious leaders of the day were often set on outward religious displays. Jesus goes after the heart and what is going on inside that leads to actions. God knows the heart and it is His grace that purifies our hearts so that we can walk with Him. In turn, we shall see God face to face for eternity.

The connection between purity and relationship makes sense even on a human level. If I have something against you or intend to harm you in any way, then that would be an obvious disruption of the relationship. So, it is in our relationship with God, an impure heart disrupts the relationship whereas a pure heart promotes intimacy and fellowship.

— "Blessed are the peacemakers, for they shall be called sons of God." (Matthew 5:9)

We don't want to ignore conflict but to bring reconciliation in disagreements. A conflict may be as small as a spat between roommates or as large as a lawsuit against one another. The reason why Christians are called to play the role of peacemaker is because our Father is a peacemaker—"for they shall be called sons of God." Like Father, like son. In our sin, we were in rebellion against God; and while we were still in sin and hostility against Him, He sent His Son, Jesus, to die for us. Now, as children who have been reconciled, we strive to imitate the reconciling love of our Father.

It's not always easy because we either want to run away from conflict or deal with it by attacking. *Let's hear it for another round of conflict resolution!* No thanks. Let's go to our corners or punch and run. But the way forward is the gospel. As people who have been reconciled to God through Jesus, we now move in the direction of reconciliation and restoration.

— "Blessed are you when others revile you and persecute you and utter all kinds of evil against you falsely on my account. Rejoice and be glad, for your reward is great in heaven, for so they persecuted the prophets who were before you." (Matthew 5:11–12)

Our modern society's response to followers of Jesus is often filled with false accusations and persecution. The range of opposition can be from being falsely accused at work because someone doesn't like Christians to being beheaded for converting to Christ. Either way, when opposition comes, it should lead to rejoicing because "your reward is great in heaven" and you are associated with "the prophets who were before you." There is a great reward coming for those who stand firm in the faith and press on through opposition.

Most of us are not familiar with physical persecution, but it's important for us to have an affinity with those who are. When we are around them, it emboldens us to stand firm in Christ, and to speak and live no matter what. My previous hairdresser was from Iran and she always had stories of persecution. One day, she introduced me to one of her friends who was from Iran and came in to get her hair done. Her dad was a pastor and he was on a hit list to be killed. Even though he pastored a church in Chicago, he was a target as well as his church. These were real threats as several people were just killed in a church in Iran and the threat was to now kill in Chicago. But the threats were not going to deter them from meeting. That night was the start of their Christmas, and they were going to have a service at midnight. I asked to pray for her and her dad. So right there in the salon with her cape on and hair color in, I prayed.

When I finished, she asked if I wanted to come to church that night. I was stuck and didn't say anything as I pondered if I wanted to face the possibility of dying that night. My hairdresser rescued me and said, "He's got kids; he can't go." I went along with it and moved on to get my haircut. Basically, my hairdresser was saying I have kids to care for, so I don't have time to go; but I was thinking I have kids, so I don't want to get killed, as if kids would exempt me from suffering. Why would that be an excuse? "God, I've got kids, so I will have to sit this one out."

My new friend along with her dad certainly wouldn't think having a family would exempt one from suffering. She said that it's normal for Christian families in Iran to have at least three to five people in their sphere of relationships that have been killed for following Christ. We need to interact with people like that. They stir us up to obedience and bold witness right here. There must be no excuse not to speak up and live in the gospel—not our family, good relations with the neighbors, or financial security. Sometimes distinct living with engagement under the reign of God will have a response of opposition. Rejoice and be glad!

CREATED FOR THE WEIGHTY LIFE

These Beatitudes demonstrate a picture of the elements of those who live under the lordship of King Jesus. These characteristics were given to us by grace and are continually formed in us by grace. Great blessings await us as we walk in the standards of the kingdom. This is a life of substance, purpose, and meaning under the reign of Christ. This is the weighty life. This is what we have been created for. And when we build our lives on these elements, the weighty life is on display for the glory of God.

One of the ways that Jesus followed up the Beatitudes was to say, "In the same way, let your light shine before others, so that they may see your good works and give glory to your Father who is in heaven" (Matthew 5:16). Good works spring from these foundational elements. The Christian life is more than our private devotional lives and our corporate worship services. We are called to engage the world and let our light shine by doing good works. The good works produced in us by grace come from God; therefore all the praise goes to Him.

You have been created for good works. Ephesians 2:10 says, "For we are his workmanship, created in Christ Jesus for good works, which God prepared beforehand, that we should walk in them." Just as you see those in the New Testament doing good works, so you have been created to do good works. In my line of work, I meet with all types of missionaries who have done amazing works for the Lord all over the world. Talking to people like that fires me up. But a common misconception is that the radical work of God overseas cannot be duplicated in America—that somehow the sacrifices, prayers, and steps of faith are only for those overseas. That those of us on American soil are destined for the rut of apathy. Don't believe it! The same God who uses people around the world also wants to use you here. God has called and crafted you to have maximum impact for His glory right here, right now.

LGDs

Farm life has been quite an adjustment for us after spending our entire lives in the city. One of the many challenges is trying to figure out how to care for the animals. There are a couple of calves in our pasture that we transported to the farm in the back of our minivan. I'm not even sure that was legal, but this is Arkansas, so I'm sure I'm safe. In addition, we have these fainting goats that fall over at the drop off a hat. And then there is the random assortment of chickens where one batch serves us by laying eggs and the other by eating ticks. It's been quite an adventure to figure out how to feed, vet, and basically keep the animals alive.

We have two outdoor dogs that are Great Pyrenees and LGDs. You know what that means? Livestock guardian dogs or LGDs. It's who they are by nature. They will just sit and watch the animals and bark at threats. But one day, our baby goat was killed by a coyote. It was a devastating and gruesome death in our young lives as farmers. My wife said, "This just got real." Where were the LGDs? They were just lounging around asleep in our front yard. They were soaking up the sun and taking it easy. While they were relaxing, our baby goat was ripped to shreds. They were created to guard the livestock and because they failed to do their jobs, a goat lost its life.

WAKE UP

In the same way, you have been created in Christ Jesus to do good works. You are not here to kick back and take it easy, because when you do, others suffer.

- ○ Jews headed to slaughter during the holocaust as the church was sleeping and afraid of persecution.
- ○ Thousands of children languish in foster care today while God's people nap and ignore mercy.
- ○ Slavery and discrimination still flourish as many believers abdicate their pursuit of righteousness and fail to mourn.
- ○ The lost perish while the Body of Christ would rather take it easy than function as peacemakers and see others reconciled to God.

When the church sleeps, others suffer. You are not here to have all the fun you can, because, when you do, others are not served and God does not receive the glory. Wake up! You have been created to thrive in the fullness of the weighty life for the benefit of others and for the glory of God. Let your light shine! God has called and crafted you to have maximum impact for His glory right here, right now.

Virtues

Farming is much harder than I thought. The idea seems cool and it's kind of hip to live on a hobby farm. Raise your own livestock, grow your own food, and, if you are really into it, you can make your own soap and clothes. Trendy stores sell farmhouse decorations and furniture while TV shows, books, and magazines display the adventure in all its glory. But it's actually hard work raising animals, feeding them morning and night, giving shots, and even castrating certain animals (I did two calves). The soil to grow food doesn't always want to cooperate; and here in our part of Arkansas, it is filled with rock, so we call it "Rockansas." The water is from a well, the sewer is on a septic tank, and the Internet is spotty. But when I tell people that we live on a farm, they think it is the coolest thing ever. And it certainly is, as long as you don't have to do any of the farming stuff!

The stuff in the Bible is amazing as well. Almost everyone in the church is blown away by the person and work of Jesus. The Bible is revered as a book without errors that tells us all we need for godliness as well as for daily life.

Each week around the country, many churches have strong biblical preachers, worship is off the charts, the programs are top notch, and the fellowship is tight knit. But when it comes time to go out and farm and live out the gospel in the land, that's altogether another story. It's hard to farm and live out the faith. People are difficult, we can be difficult; circumstances are messy, we can be messy; the world can be hard, we can be hard; and life can be draining, confusing, and discouraging. And we can find ourselves drained, confused, and discouraged. Just as it's a lot easier to talk about farming than to actually farm, so it's a lot easier to just talk about living the Christian life than it is to actually live the Christian life.

But what if I could convince you that in the midst of all those difficulties, you are not alone? I'm not talking about God's omnipresence or Jesus' promise to be with you always, which are both true. But you are not alone in the sense that God lives inside of you. You have the Holy Spirit of God living in you on Sunday and every day of the week. The Holy Spirit—the third Person of the Trinity—who stirs you to live out the Christian life on Sunday—is the same Person who empowers you to live such a life throughout the week. There can and should be congruency in the talk and the walk. In fact, the outward display of an inward transformation is mandatory in the commands of the Bible, and it is carried out by the very One who commanded it. In other words, God performs what He commands through the power of the Holy Spirit living out His life through you.

FULL STRENGTH, FULL DEPENDENCE

An internal to external manifestation of the weighty life comes from a display of virtues called the fruit of the Spirit. Believers are commanded to "walk by the Spirit" as opposed to the trivial nature of carrying out "the desires of the flesh" (Galatians 5:16). Those who walk by the Spirit, in submission to God and His ways, will display the fruit of the Spirit. Galatians 5:22–23 states: "But the fruit of the Spirit is love, joy, peace, patience, kindness, goodness, faithfulness, gentleness, self-control; against such things there is no law." And, believe it or not, this is a package deal where the Holy Spirit produces all these virtues in a believer, not just one or two. It's not about your ability or inability but the Holy Spirit of God enabling you to display these virtues in your life *on a daily basis.*

How? It's one of full strength and full dependence. You have a responsibility to love others, to be patient, and to exhibit self-control. You are commanded to live the weighty life in all of these virtues. At the same time, you realize you can't pull it off on your own, so you fully depend upon the Lord. You work with all your might to produce fruit, and at the same time you depend on the Lord to pull it off. It's not that you do your part and God does His part, but it's all God's part and power that you live into.

When I lived in Chicago, I commuted to work year-round on a Raleigh Detour bicycle. It was partly for my mental health so that I could fight back against the cold, depressing winters. I thought I was tough biking in the cold, snow, and ice. My plan was to transition to Arkansas and commute the same way. One major problem: the hills are brutal. My round-trip commute in Chicago was one hour, but my round trip in Arkansas was two hours. Some of the hills were so difficult that I had to walk my bike to the top.

After six months of fighting the hills, I was able to shave significant time off the commute. It wasn't because I got stronger or adopted some new training regimen. It's because I got a new bike, the same brand and model as my previous bike, a Raleigh Detour. But the new bike had one major difference, it was electric. You really can't understand an electric bike until you ride one. My bike has something called pedal assist. You have to start pedaling, but it's as if some mysterious power takes over and propels the bike forward in power and strength. It looks as if I'm cranking up those hills, but it's the power of the bike that is taking over.

Paul experienced this as he wrote in Colossians 1:29, "For this I toil, struggling with all his energy that he powerfully works within me." This is the imagery of fighting and contending in praying, preaching, evangelism, refuting false teaching, and rebuking others. The fact that Paul struggles and strives doesn't mean that it is done in his own energy. Human effort doesn't mean that God is absent, nor does God's power exclude human effort. Paul works hard and recognizes that it is God's energy through him. There is full strength and full dependence.

THE FRUIT OF THE SPIRIT

The fruit of the Spirit is a package deal where the Holy Spirit desires to produce all these virtues in your life so that you can live the weighty life for the glory of God. Just as with the Beatitudes, the fruit of the Spirit is laid out in a list form: "Love, joy, peace . . ." It's not a checklist but a list that is helpful for self-examination. I find it revealing to pick out each virtue, one at a time, to see the evidence or lack of evidence of the fruit in my life. The purpose is to pinpoint an area where I may need to give extra time and focused prayer to see the virtue manifested in my life.

We could fly all over the Bible and find teachings and examples connected to each virtue. We could drill down and do a lengthy study on every virtue, but let's just quickly scroll through them.

—Love

"Love is patient and kind . . ." So begins the classic description of love from 1 Corinthians 13. The descriptors of love in this chapter are not to be sentimental and destined for a picture on your wall or the typical Hallmark card. How do you love someone who won't get it together? Love is always about a selfless sacrifice where it's not about you, and it's probably going to hurt. How do you love instead of burning with jealousy (1 Corinthians 13:4)? How do you love instead of bragging and boasting about your accomplishments (1 Corinthians 13:4)? How do you love when you want to pursue your own rights or agenda (1 Corinthians 13:5)?

How do you love without getting provoked and irritated (1 Corinthians 13:5)? How do you love instead of becoming resentful (1 Corinthians 13:5)?

It's clear that the call to love is not sappy but sacrificial. Again, it's not about you, and it's probably going to hurt. And this virtue, as well as the fruit, is only possible because God has sacrificially loved you and now empowers you to sacrificially love others. Often, love won't feel good; instead, it can be challenging and difficult. In fact, I'm learning that in order to truly love I have to set my own agenda aside in order to benefit others.

My youngest child is nine. He has a variety of challenges that, at times, can be exhausting, and it feels like they will never end. Weekends are the worst because he is not in school. Like a marathon, these challenges can be draining and hard. There have been times he has commanded all my attention, but I have often viewed him as an interruption to my goals. It's like I want to get on the Internet to search for "greatness," but our son is wandering onto the street. I want to sit down and read the *Wall Street Journal* (like all great leaders), but he starts to scream because he has wedged himself in a chair and become stuck for the hundredth time. He is an interruption to my accomplishing "great things." Or, is he a part of God's plan for me to love? In the same way, God has given you people to love in your life right now. You may view them as interruptions to your plans and pursuits. However, they are not an interruption but the main goal for you to sacrificially love. God uses these challenges as a means to draw you down the path of the weighty life.

—Joy

Sustainable happiness in the Lord is a good description of joy. But it's often not a description of my life, and at times seems unattainable. Here is a recurring scenario. Something in life makes me happy. For example, I'm filled with joy when biking in the sunshine, or I feel upbeat after an effective day at work, or I'm in a good mood after a date with my wife or some fun time with my kids. There are things in life that make me joyful and happy. Yet, I quickly let circumstances or people steal my joy. A road closes down for two months so I can't bike to work and I'm mad. At times my wrist, heel, or back are acting up and I'm bummed. Often someone's complaining and it annoys me. The bottom line is this: It doesn't take much to steal my joy. It's like I'm sitting around the campfire singing, "I've got the joy, joy, joy, joy down in my heart . . ." Then some disgruntled person comes along and drenches my fire, and it's gone. Happens all the time!

Yet, the Bible says, "Rejoice always" (1 Thessalonians 5:16). You are not called to be happy, joyful, and rejoicing just for the sake of being happy, joyful, and rejoicing. It's not joy for joy's sake, but finding joy in the object—the Lord. The Lord is to be the object of your ultimate happiness, joy, and rejoicing.

This kind of joy doesn't terminate on you, but it has a dual purpose: It gives you sustained happiness and it allows you to serve others. That's the kind of joy you want, sustained in God alone, a quality that at the same time empowers you to love others, no matter who they are or what they are going through. You know that you are experiencing this Holy Spirit-produced joy when you start to see that people and circumstances can't take it away. It's a locked-in and sustainable joy in the Lord.

──Peace

All true believers have peace with God. Prior to conversion, humans were internally warring against God. Jesus came to reconcile God and humans through His death on the cross and His resurrection. Through faith in Jesus, we are reconciled with God and are at peace with Him. You may describe your conversion experience as one of peace because you are no longer fighting against God; His wrath is no longer aimed in your direction, for now there is a relationship of peace through Jesus.

Though we have peace with God, we can still be characterized by anxiety, worry, and restlessness. God's Word tells us not to be anxious but to be prayerful and thankful and in turn ". . . the peace of God, which surpasses all understanding, will guard your hearts and your minds in Christ Jesus" (Philippians 4:7). The peace talked about here is a tranquil state, an inner rest, and let me go so far as to say a *feeling* of calm that God provides. Part of the peace is the very presence of the God of peace (Philippians 4:9, ". . . and the God of peace will be with you."). Life can be raging, but you're not. Life can be screaming, but you are calm. Things look hopeless, but you are hopeful in God. You have a disposition that is confident in God and His control.

I can't give you a full breakdown of this peace or even explain it because it is the "peace of God, which surpasses all understanding." This is a peace produced by the Holy Spirit; this is the peace of God. It is a peace that "will guard your hearts and your minds in Christ Jesus." When Paul wrote to the Philippians, he was in prison and under guards, yet he wrote of the peace of God. God's peace is like a guard. It guards your heart and your mind so that you are protected against anxiety. God knows what He is doing, and He is here to give you His peace, no matter what is going on.

——Patience

If you have a hard time extending patience to others, then you should remember about how God is patient with you. Paul puts it this way in 1 Timothy 1:15–16:

> *The saying is trustworthy and deserving of full acceptance, that Christ Jesus came into the world to save sinners, of whom I am the foremost. But I received mercy for this reason, that in me, as the foremost, Jesus Christ might display his perfect patience as an example to those who were to believe in him for eternal life.*

You and I are a target of God's patience. In turn, we can now be patient with others.

There are also other areas where we can exhibit patience. Maybe it's waiting on God's timing. You are tired of waiting for a breakthrough that never seems to come, and it's wearing on you. You can rest and wait on God and His good sovereign plan to unfold. Maybe you are impatient with yourself as your own issues get old. It seems as though you are never going to grow but keep doing the same foolish things. By God's grace, you can forget the past and press on in Christ and His transformative power. Maybe you are suffering in your body and mind while waiting for the next test or result. May you set your hope on the Lord who cares for you and will comfort you in the present, and will one day alleviate your suffering forever. The weighty life is a patient life.

—Kindness

Since God has a habit of kindness toward you, with the Spirit's empowerment you can have a habit of kindness toward others. The weighty life is filled with kindness. I find it helpful to look at the kindness in other Christ-followers and seek to imitate it in a variety of ways.

One of the kindest persons I have ever met was a woman named Kae. We refer to her as the kids' California grandma and her husband Steve is the grandpa, and we have called them both Nani and Papi. Right after marriage we moved from Texas to Santa Monica, California. Somehow, we came into contact with Kae, and she embraced us. She was so kind in sending us cards all the time with detailed notes inside. She would also send us books with beautiful handwritten letters on the cover. Then we had our first child and there were complications at birth. But Kae was there not only with a basket of goodies for the baby but the best matzah ball soup you have ever tasted, with huge matzah balls. Once our stove went out in our house, so she bought us a new one (and she was not wealthy).

When we had our second child, she loved her the same way as the first. Kae would buy her American Girl dolls and even took her to Disneyland. She really was their California grandma. A month before we moved away from California, we had our daughter Jordan, and it just fit to give her the middle name Kae. Kae was one of the kindest people we have ever known. She embodied kindness and just let it spontaneously spill out onto many people. She was gripped by the kindness of God and displayed it to others. Now she is with the Lord. And from time to time, we still connect with her husband, Papi, and share great memories of Nani and her kindness that is worthy of imitation.

—Goodness

In wrapping up the letter to the Galatians, Paul writes in 6:10, "So then, as we have opportunity, let us do good to everyone, and especially to those who are of the household of faith." This goodness is to be aimed at the world and the church. As you express goodness to the world, it plays out in the way you love your community and those in your spheres of influence. Of course, this means verbally sharing the gospel, but it also means specific works of good. Often this will express itself in a burden you have for the world. I tend to think that the burden is from God, and He has written into His playbook specific good works He wants you to do. Maybe you have a burden to serve refugees, widows, orphans, the unborn, those with disabilities, the poor, addicts, the homeless, etc. Maybe you want to work for the common good in the political realm or in the arts or a neighborhood safety program. You don't have to start your own nonprofit or turn it into a program, but you simply use your gifts and time to do good.

We are to do good to all but "especially to those who are of the household of faith." You are to lean in the direction of the church. There are many opportunities to do good to one another through encouragement, exhortation, financial help, emotional support, and generally being there and sacrificing for one another. This nonprogrammed and informal ministry goes on all the time. Yet, there are the more organized and programmed ways of doing good—whether leading a small group, teaching children and serving in media, or logistics. In programmed and nonprogrammed ways, you can do good to the household of faith.

——Faithfulness

Hebrews 10:36, "For you have need of endurance, so that when you have done the will of God, you may receive what is promised." Your great need is to press on in faithfulness in doing the will of God. You may think that your greatest need is healing, a perfect marriage, supportive adult kids, or a comfortable and secure life. But your greatest need is to press on, no matter what happens.

Is there a certain area of your life where you need to press on in faithfulness? Maybe it's an area where you have been kind of flakey—not following through or slacking off or abdicating responsibilities. Flakiness embodies the trivial life while faithfulness demonstrates the weighty life. Maybe you need to move from flakiness to faithfulness.

○ Maybe you have stopped loving and leading your family spiritually. Get back at it!

○ Maybe you have stopped leading yourself, and your time with the Lord, in prayer and in the Word, has vanished. Get in the Word!

○ Maybe you have been a flake at church. Follow through!

○ Maybe it's an area of sin where you used to be more vigilant and now your guard is down. Get it back up!

In all of these areas you may blame shift and give long explanations for being flakey. But it's time to press on in faithfulness. Let your flakiness end right now. May you cry out for God to exhibit His fruit of the Spirit through you so that you move from flakey to faithful.

—Gentleness

At times, around my family, I am anything but gentle. I want to grow *big time* in this area. It's like I need an entire overhaul to impact my head, heart, and hands. I want my mind transformed, my heart changed, and my hands to do good works. I want a humble mind, tender heart, and gentle hands. Rather than just say, "Be gentle," I want to go in for an overhaul of my head, heart, and hands. I want the fruit of the Spirit of gentleness to be evident in my life in all that I think, feel, and do.

I look to Jesus for my change toward gentleness. Jesus is not asking you and me to fix ourselves, but He asks us to come to Him all messed up and mean, and to find His gentle forgiveness. On the cross, He bore our anger and wrath as the anger and wrath of the Father was poured out on Him instead of on us. Maybe you have a hard time being gentle. There is a common phrase that says, "Those who are wounded wound others." But I think we all have been wounded and we all wound others. Thankfully, Jesus is gentle with us and offers forgiveness and change. Go in for the overhaul, and may you find your heart tender, your mind humble, and your hands gentle.

──Self-Control

The apostle Paul once instructed his coworker, Titus, how to lead the churches in Crete. In Titus 2, Paul addresses the need for self-control in different groups within the church. He wants the older men to exhibit self-control by being faithful (Titus 2:2). This is not the time in their life to be out of control with money, drinking, or sex. The older women were to be self-controlled in their speech and their drinking (Titus 2:3). They weren't to sit around gossiping and getting drunk. The younger women were to be self-controlled so they could love those closest to them (Titus 2:4). They weren't to go out and "find themselves" through indulgence but simply to love. Then he says that the young men need to be urged to be "self-controlled" (Titus 2:6). Young men have a tendency to be all over the place in crazy living. They really needed self-control, as do all of us.

Sometimes, sin seems so valuable that you are unwilling to let go and walk away. The common areas of struggle with self-control are in the areas of spending money, eating issues, laziness or wasting time, anger or out-of-control speech, sexual immorality, the abuse of drugs (legal or illegal) or alcohol, and a sinful thought life. There are various trivial patterns that may seem impossible to escape, but we know that through Christ there is a way of escape. It's important to keep in mind that you not only escape but you continue to train yourself so that you can escape over and over again.

Think about training for a moment. One year I went to my first and only golf tournament at the BMW Championship in Lake Forest. These best golfers in the world were amazing with the control they had over the little ball. They train constantly to control their shots. The most famous person there was Tiger Woods. You may know that, while he was at the top of his game, he had some personal areas of his life that were out of control. So as he kept training to be a better golfer, his private world fell apart. As Christians, we can do the same thing. You are training or have trained to be at the top of your game in some aspect. You have invested your time to be excellent, but there may be an area of your life that is out of control. You need to redirect your training efforts. You need to focus on the grace of Jesus to give you self-control in your personal life. This is where you let the Word change your affections, spend time in prayer asking God to change you, and call out to other people to keep you accountable.

AGRITAINMENT

You could take these nine virtues and literally cultivate them the rest of your life. If you see some indicators of fruit in your life, be encouraged. If you see a lack of some of these virtues, don't give up. The Holy Spirit of God lives in you, and He wants to produce His fruit in your life. But bearing fruit will take your whole focus; it can't be something you dabble in from time to time.

You need to be careful of "entertainment farming." Entertainment farming, also known as *agritainment*, is when small farmers turn part of their farms into entertainment attractions. Farming is hard work and it can be difficult to make a living off the farm, so they focus on entertainment farming. They create pumpkin patches, corn mazes, pony rides, and bounce houses. My family loves these places. The small farmers may still do a little farming on the side, but they are making money doing entertainment farming.

If you are not careful, you may take the main thing of bearing fruit and make it a side thing while focusing on entertainment farming, which is really the "works of the flesh" (Galatians 5:19). When we make our lives all about making money, having elite families, comfort, focusing exclusively on our sports, crafts, vacations, and having me-centered fun, then we have shifted to entertainment farming. But we are people of the Holy Spirit. Our main purpose is to bear fruit for the glory of God. We need to be careful that we don't make cultivating and bearing fruit a side business of our lives.

May your life be one of full strength and full dependence upon the Spirit of God to produce His fruit in you. I have found it helpful to express my need for God's help to bear fruit through a daily prayer written by the godly theologian, John Stott. I have it in my Bible and try to pray it each morning. Make this your prayer before the Lord.

Heavenly Father, I pray that this day I may live in your presence and please you more and more.

Lord Jesus, I pray that this day I may take up my cross and follow you.

Holy Spirit, I pray that this day you will fill me with yourself and cause your fruit to ripen in my life: love, joy, peace, patience, kindness, goodness, faithfulness, gentleness and self-control.[1]

---

1. Prayer by John Stott, teaching by Christopher Wright, https://www.youtube.com/watch?v=Wv46pnDvhzs, 9aday: Becoming Like Jesus. 9 Fruit of the Spirit - #1 Introduction. Series by the Langham Partnership, www.langham.org. Published 12/4/2012.

Norms

Our firstborn son came into the world on November 12, 1998, in Santa Monica, California. Six months later, we were pregnant with our first daughter. A lot of people, inside and outside the church, were passing judgment on us in subtle and not-so-subtle ways. "You do know how that happens don't you?" Ha! Ha! Very funny, I've never heard that one. "How many kids are you going to have?" There literally were more dogs in Santa Monica than kids. We had clearly broken some unspoken rule by having not only one but two children and so close together. A few years later we broke the rules again and had another child. "I can't believe you are having so many kids. Don't you feel like you are going to neglect each child with so many kids—besides, what about population control?"

One month after the birth of our third child, we moved out of the "no kid zone" into a much more kid-friendly environment in Chicago. Our fourth child was born a few years later without the drama and with plenty of support. We had a large family but still within the bounds of what was culturally appropriate. However, we were about to break the rules all over again but in a new way. The Lord led us to adopt a child from Ethiopia. Most of our friends were supportive but there were new challengers on the scene. "Do you really think it is appropriate to bring a black child into a white family? You could mess them up for life. Besides, how do you know the child wasn't abducted and sold to the highest bidder?" We pushed through the naysayers and brought home our sweet girl who has been such a delight.

Nine months later we entered the foster care system and welcomed a little boy into our family. This action triggered the "adoption police." That's what I pejoratively call these so-called defenders of orphans who have rules and codes that one must not break. We had clearly stepped over the line in pursuing a child so close in age to our newly adopted daughter, and besides, we weren't equipped to handle all the emotional trauma that was sure to come. But we pushed through it all, and after forty-four months as foster parents, we legally adopted our son.

Yet, there was something we were concealing during this time from most people because we were sick and tired of all the judgment being thrown our way. Right in the midst of pursuing our Ethiopia adoption and foster care, we were also applying to adopt in Jamaica. Through a series of starts and stops, we finally adopted our son from Jamaica seven years later. It was clearly a miracle. That would be a total of seven children.

The most common pushback we hear is along the lines of, "When is enough, enough? You already have seven kids!

When is enough, enough?" The world would classify our family size as reckless and irresponsible. Some in the church judge it as bad stewardship or an attention-getting ploy. Still other believers would be more positive by calling us radical or crazy sold out for Jesus. But we don't see it as reckless or radical, but normal. God calls children a blessing,

> *Behold, children are a heritage from the LORD,*
> *the fruit of the womb a reward.*
> *. . . Blessed is the man who fills his quiver with them!*
> (Psalm 127:3–5)

I don't know about you, but I've never found anyone trying to restrict the blessings of God in their lives. Of course, I don't really mean the more children, the more blessings, but I kind of do. Each child is a unique gift and blessing. You also don't have to have children to be blessed as there are many avenues to blessing. My point is that our large family should not be viewed as abnormal but normal according to the Word of God. God calls children a gift and a reward, so we are agreeing with Him by having children all for His glory. That's not reckless or radical but normal. Let's call it a weighty norm. By God's grace, we are aligning ourselves with what brings a blessing our way and glory God's way.

In addition, it's part of the weighty norms for Christians to welcome the vulnerable into their lives and homes. It's not about works righteousness or showy advocacy, but simply hearing the Word and doing it. James 1:27 states:

"Religion that is pure and undefiled before God the Father is this: to visit orphans and widows in their affliction, and to keep oneself unstained from the world." There is nothing reckless or radical in caring for the vulnerable. It's not heroic but normal. The weighty norms of the Kingdom of God should consistently be in play in the lives of all believers. It's just normal.

WEIGHTY NORMS

The Bible is filled with a vision of God's people functioning in such a way that they are turning their backs on the trivial life and living in the fullness of the weighty life. The world may call it reckless and foolhardy. Even some within the church may say these weighty norms are for fully committed and zealous believers, but that it's not normative. Are we reading out of the same Bible? Consider a snapshot of the early church in Acts 2. The life of these believers is both descriptive and prescriptive. It describes what the early church looked like while advocating the normalcy of their experience for the whole church moving forward. In other words, the rest of the New Testament confirms and affirms the weighty norms of the early church for us today.

Acts 2 portrays the day of Pentecost where Peter preached the gospel of Jesus Christ to Jews from all around the world. About three thousand people repented of their sin and were baptized (Acts 2:41). The book of Acts starts out mentioning 120 believers (Acts 1:15) but now we have more than three thousand. Talk about massive church growth and revival! There are enough new believers to make up a small town. What happens next? Weighty norms. The church falls into normal patterns of biblical living that may seem radical to us, but that were just normal to them.

DEVOTED FELLOWSHIP

Acts 2:42 tells us that the people of the early church "devoted themselves to the apostles' teaching and the fellowship, to the breaking of bread and the prayers." Not only were they devoted to Jesus, but they were devoted to His church. They were all-in devoted to Jesus and all-in devoted to His church. It was normal for them to do life together in their praying, feasting, and spreading the gospel. They were not isolated Christians but a community of believers moving in the same direction for the glory of God.

God may be doing some great things in your life, but it's not just about your individualized spirituality. You are to be an intimate part of the Body of Christ. The church's fellowship and life together should go so far as to function as family members relate to one another. The Body of Christ is your family. As natural families participate in life together, such is the case of your new spiritual family. Devotion to one another on this level may seem a bit extreme, but it was normal to the early Christian believers.

COMPLETE ADHERENCE

Another part of their devotion was to the apostles' teaching, which points to the Word of God. It's extreme in our generation to say that we are people devoted to God's Word. People may be fine if you are devoted to God, but it's taking it too far when you also say you are devoted to His Word. Yet, God can't be separated from His Word because in His Word He reveals who He is. The culture may call that extreme, but it's simply the normal Christian life. True believers take all of God's Word without picking and choosing certain verses to keep while ignoring others. It's all from God and for your benefit, so pay attention to it all (2 Timothy 3:16). Devotion to God's Word is not reckless or radical but part of the weighty norms.

EXPECTANT PRAYER

The early church was also devoted to prayer, and miracles started to happen. Acts 2:43 records how ". . . awe came upon every soul, and many wonders and signs were being done through the apostles." As the church prayed, the Lord worked signs and wonders that confirmed the apostles' teaching. Often, we want to debate whether or not miracles happen in a similar way today. Rather than dive into a full-blown explanation filled with arguments and counterarguments, let's go in a different direction. I'm just wondering, if the miracles that were normative in the early church seem to be absent today, could it be that the *prayers* that were normative in the early church are absent as well? The church often does a poor job in praying too little and too lame. We don't spend much time in prayer, and when we finally get around to it, we don't expect much.

May the Lord stir us to be more prayerful and expectant— not expectant in the sense of an absolute guarantee but in prayer with hopeful expectation. It should be normal for you to spend time in prayer and actually believe that God will answer your prayer. Be bold and branch out and ask for God to move in mighty and powerful ways. "Whatever you ask in my name, this I will do, that the Father may be glorified in the Son. If you ask me anything in my name, I will do it" (John 14:13–14). Prayers in line with God's kingdom bring answers where God gets all the glory. This kind of praying may seem extreme or radical, but for the early church it was normal.

SACRIFICIAL SERVING

One of the most striking weighty norms of the early church was the devotion shown in caring for one another. "And all who believed were together and had all things in common" (Acts 2:44). It's lip service to speak of being all in with community as long as money is left out of the conversation— but not in the early church. They were together and, in some sense, their money was together and available to those who had a need. "And they were selling their possessions and belongings and distributing the proceeds to all, as any had need" (Acts 2:45). This wasn't mandatory but, rather, was an overflow of love. They saw people with a genuine need, and they responded in love.

> *Now the full number of those who believed were of one heart and soul, and no one said that any of the things that belonged to him was his own, but they had everything in common. And with great power the apostles were giving their testimony to the resurrection of the Lord Jesus, and great grace was upon them all. There was not a needy person among them, for as many as were owners of lands or houses sold them and brought the proceeds of what was sold and laid it at the apostles' feet, and it was distributed to each as any had need.*
>
> (Acts 4:32–35)

Did you catch that in verse 34? "There was not a needy person among them . . ." Can you imagine a church functioning where we say, "There will never be a needy person among us"? That seems reckless to some while radical to others, but for the early church it was normal.

In the past, there were strong movements that combined gospel preaching with care for the poor. The Salvation Army used to have a strong history of giving out the gospel and making provision for people physically. Some of these movements even exist today where it is all about caring for those in need, both in the church and outside the church. Programs and movements are great but that doesn't mean that you as an individual can take a pass while occasionally dropping in to feed the homeless or packing a care box at Christmas. All good, but that's just dabbling in meeting needs when you could be living out the fullness of the weighty norms. Let me encourage you to focus on personal investment. Whether you go through a program or not, invest in people personally.

Mike was my best man at my wedding. Actually, my grandma was my best man, but I'll get to that in a moment. Mike made the conscious decision to get a job as a dishwasher at Baylor Hospital in Dallas. Many said he was wasting his brilliance as well as blowing all of his potential, but Mike pushed through. He went in there to preach the gospel and to understand the plight of the poor. It wasn't like a short-term mission trip or even a summer job. Mike spent twelve years washing dishes and investing in the lives of those in need. He built relationships with those who had been tossed aside—high school dropouts, ex-cons, sexual offenders, and drug addicts. Some chalked it up to insanity while others said Mike was just crazy for Jesus, but the early church would call it normal. It's just part of the weighty norms of the kingdom to invest in the needs of others for the glory of God.

Now back to my main best man, my grandma. During my twenties, I took care of my grandma as her health failed and her mind ebbed away. I'm the last person that should have taken care of her, and I didn't do it out of the kindness of my heart but out of conviction from God's Word. "But if a widow has children or grandchildren, let them first learn to show godliness to their own household and to make some return to their parents, for this is pleasing in the sight of God" (1 Timothy 5:4). The Word not only calls children to step up but also grandchildren. It may seem like a heroic thing to do but it's supposed to just be normal.

Caring for my grandma was one of the hardest things I had ever done. As a young punk I could barely take care of myself, let alone care for a fragile woman in her eighties. Beyond the feeding, dressing, and daily maintenance, there were other challenges like figuring out Medicare, navigating the various doctors, and negotiating for additional services. I was such a terrible caregiver, easily irritated with my grandma, angry at the medical system, afraid of the unknown, and even questioning why God put me into this situation. The Christian life was supposed to be hard but not this kind of hard. All I could do was cry out to God for help and then to simply show up day in and day out.

My grandma's health deteriorated to the point that she had to move into a nursing home. I soon discovered that a significant number of residents were just dumped there to end their lives all alone. It was depressing. Some relatives would pop in at Christmas but that was about it. I even heard some say of their aging parents, "I just can't see them in this state. I want to remember them as they once were." But it's not about you! I hear people give the same reason why they can't do foster care. "I just don't want to get close and have to see the kids go back. It's just too much." But it's not about you! Loving and serving others is not about how it makes you feel. Too many times people give to a charity or even go on a short-term mission trip to feel good about themselves. It's almost as if they are trying to justify their trivial life by giving occasional nods to the weighty life.

Thankfully, I saw some refusing to default to the trivial life and were aggressively bringing glory to God in the midst of dim circumstances. Iris was the woman I told you about earlier who wrote to me several years later to update me on her work with the residents and to let me know that all had forgotten me. But I have not forgotten her, as she was consistently making the rounds and loving the residents. Her sidekick was a woman named Daisy who listened to the stories of the elderly and even showed up to their funerals when no one else was around. There were many other servants living the normal Christian life. They even loaded up a bus full of residents and took a field trip to my wedding. Right next to me was my grandma in her wheelchair. What a moment! The world might call this a nice sentimental story, and others may see it as a unique noble work, but God calls it normal. It's part of the weighty norms of the kingdom to personally invest in those in need for the glory of God.

CONSISTENT PROCLAMATION

It was normal for the early church to spread the gospel and see others come to Christ. "And day by day, attending the temple together and breaking bread in their homes, they received their food with glad and generous hearts, praising God and having favor with all the people. And the Lord added to their number day by day those who were being saved" (Acts 2:46–47). As they were meeting, worshiping, praying, and caring for one another, people were getting saved. The gospel was being preached and God kept adding more and more people.

God desires to add to His church, and He wants His people devoted to preaching the gospel. How are you doing with sharing the good news with others and desiring them to come to know and follow Jesus? I'm not content or satisfied with my inconsistent proclamation. I'm just wondering, again, if the conversions that were normative in the early church seem to be absent today. It could be that the gospel proclamation that was normative in the early church is absent as well. I want this lack of gospel sharing to disturb you as it disturbs me. Out of love for God and a love for others, we want to share our faith so that others can be saved. It's not just delegated to missionaries, pastors, or evangelists but to all believers. We have a story to tell of how the good news has invaded our lives. It's part of the weighty norms for the gospel to be shared so that others can be saved, and God glorified.

YES, BUT . . .

All of this may seem aspirational though unattainable. Maybe it's just "pie in the sky" or some utopian dream totally disconnected from reality. Not at all. The New Testament doesn't describe a sinless community free from fault with ever-ascending perfection. Just three chapters later, we peek inside the church to see Ananias and Sapphira struck dead for deception and greed (Acts 5:1–11). Read on, and you will see that the early church often went off the rails theologically; some were sexually deviant, others slipped into idolatry, and the divisions and conflicts were rampant. They still had their fair share of the trivial life. But Jesus' teaching and the apostles' instruction always aimed at the weighty life. And though we will never completely bring glory to God until we are with Him in eternity, we nevertheless press on in the weighty norms by His grace and His power.

Some may say that this kind of living is not sustainable and leads to burnout. That's a fair assessment that requires a couple of responses. First, you can burn out if you are running in your own strength and power, disconnected from Christ-centered community. If you are separated from other believers, you are liable to run when you need to rest or to push forward when you need to pull back. You need the consistent input of others to not only spur you on to love and good deeds, but also to take seasons of rest and refreshment. Let community be your encouragement and your protection as you live out the weighty life.

Another important way to sustain the weighty life is to recognize it as faithful plodding in the weighty norms. Most of what you do will not be a grand leap of faith followed by the next grand leap of faith. It's a few risks here and there, but mainly it's about showing up in the mundane happenings of life. The act of adoption takes an initial risk, but it's followed by daily faithfulness to raise the child. Being bold with the gospel is exciting when you see someone commit to Christ, but daily discipleship requires ongoing attention and time. Saying yes to serve in your local church is a big deal, but the follow-up will require you to follow through on your commitments. Opening up your spare bedroom to a recovering addict is a big step, but the daily grind of helping him put his life back together requires consistency. Committing to care for aging parents is God honoring, but the road ahead will call for faithfulness even in their decline. The initial faith commitment must always be followed by continual faithfulness.

And lest you think that the weighty life is reserved for middle- to upper-class Westerners with excessive time, money, and margin, then you need to get out more. I've seen the weighty life all around. I've caught glimpses of it in Ethiopia from the bathroom attendants giving praise to God while handing out paper towels for spare change, all the way to college students scraping by in order to work for the good of the society. The weighty norms are often on display in the Ethiopian family of faith as the older ones care for the vulnerable young, while the young return the favor and care for the suffering old.

Then there was the driver we met in Jamaica with a kind disposition. He takes advantage of every break to devour the Word of God and give God the glory. Jamaican shopkeepers gather early in the morning for prayer and then sing hymns that echo on into eternity. Weighty norms.

The depth of destruction left by Haiti's natural disasters was shocking, but the weighty life broke through in the hospitality and love of the saints. Sacrificial giving, service, and care were put on display during the darkest of times giving glory to God.

My wife and I saw the sacrificial weighty life on full display during our foster care training on the southwest side of Chicago where many of the participants, as well as the instructors, were just scraping by, yet they were opening their homes to more and more children for the glory of God. It's just what they do.

I've seen it in rural Arkansas in the pastors who are bi-vocational in preaching the Word then going off all day to mow grass or to stay up late at night working a double shift. I'm humbled in their presence. The weighty life is the way of life everywhere that God has redeemed people for His praise and glory.

LOOKING TOWARD HOME

Over the last thirty years, I have ended my emails and letters with "Looking Toward Home." My sendoff is intentionally spiritual: Home = Heaven. My closing indicates that I'm looking toward heaven. I'm looking toward that time when we will completely escape the trivial life and live in the weighty life all for the glory of God. I'm Looking Toward Home!

Am I really? On a good day, yes, but on most days, no. More often than not, I'm grinding it out and just trying to make it through the day. I love the Lord, but I get distracted. I care for His people, but I get selfish. I strive for the weighty life, yet the default mode keeps creeping in. But every now and then, a good day will roll around. God's Word is sweet, communion in prayer is intimate, sacrificial service seems easy, and I even enjoy His people. On those days, I see the Lord and I'm ready to go *home*. But in good days and bad, God's grace is sufficient. And whether we see it or not, He's gradually stripping us of the trivial life and bringing us into the fullness of the weighty life for our good and His glory.

LOOKING TOWARD HOME,
Jason Lancaster

ABOUT THE AUTHOR

Jason Lancaster ThM (Dallas Theological Seminary), D.Min. (Trinity Evangelical Divinity School) has spent the last twenty-plus years pastoring churches in the Los Angeles (Providence Church) and Chicago (Evanston Bible Fellowship) areas helping the younger generation to launch in life. Now he ministers in a retirement community in Hot Springs Village, Arkansas, (Village Bible Church) helping people to land in life. Jason is married with seven children who are all adjusting from city life to farm life.

All royalties from this book will be given to support The Call whose goal is to mobilize the Church in Arkansas to love foster children with the extravagant love of Christ through fostering and adoption. Check them out at www. thecallinarkansas.org.

Find out more about the author by visiting:
www.thetriviallife.com

ABOUT SHEPHERD PRESS PUBLICATIONS

- They are gospel driven.
- They are heart focused.
- They are life changing.

OUR INVITATION TO YOU

We passionately believe that what we are publishing can be of benefit to you, your family, your friends, and your work colleagues. So we are inviting you to join our online mailing list so that we may reach out to you with news about our latest and forthcoming publications, and with special offers.

Visit:

www.shepherdpress.com/newsletter

and provide your name and email address.